ONE HUNDRED AND ONE METHODS

OF

COOKING POULTRY

WITH

Hints on Selection, Trussing, and Carving

By AUNT CHLOE

LONDON

J. S. VIRTUE & CO., LIMITED, 26, IVY LANE

PATERNOSTER ROW

1888

PREFACE.

AMONGST the almost countless number of books written on the subject of practical cookery, I have not yet met with one dealing exclusively with the various methods of cooking and serving poultry. This little work is sent forth for the purpose of providing, in a handy form, such information; so that when the housewife, or her cook, wishes to prepare an especially tempting dish, there will be no necessity to search through her miscellaneous cookery books in order to discover the recipe.

The recipes, which embrace all the best known and approved methods, both English and foreign, of cooking poultry, are all well tried, and reliable. Many of them are strictly original, while others are to be met with in a somewhat similar form in various cookery books, ancient and modern. These latter, however, have all been tested by the writer, and in every case varied, in order to form what she considers a better method. It is with great confidence, therefore, that she now gives them, hoping that they will prove satisfactory to all those who care to try them.

CONTENTS.

CHAPTER I.

CHAPTER II.
CHICKENS.

CHAPTER III.
DUCKS.

CHAPTER IV.
GEESE.

CHAPTER V.

TURKEYS.

CHAPTER VI.

FOWLS IN GENERAL.

CHAPTER VII.

SAUCES AND GRAVIES.

CHAPTER VIII.

ONE HUNDRED AND ONE METHODS

OF

COOKING POULTRY.

CHAPTER I.

THE SELECTION OF POULTRY FOR THE TABLE.

THE choosing of poultry intended for table purposes is a subject with which every housewife should strive to make herself familiar. It is not studied nearly so much as it ought to be, hence the keen disappointment which is often experienced by those who have purchased at random. . They are puzzled to know why the fowl, which has been so carefully cooked, should prove tough, and comparatively tasteless, instead of being, as they had expected, tender and juicy. The cause of failure undoubtedly lay in the fact of a wrong selection having been made, after which, of course, the most judicious cooking in the world would be powerless to rectify the mistake.

There are numerous books written for the guidance of those fortunate individuals who are able to rear poultry for their own use ; still, a few hints given as a result of personal experience, may not come amiss. The very best breed of all for table purposes is the Dorking; these are white-legged, large-bodied, and

B

full-breasted, and their flesh is beautifully white and delicate. Next in value comes the Creve-cœur and La Flèche, French breeds, as their names indicate. These have dark-coloured legs—the unreasonable prejudice against which, I am glad to see, is fast becoming a thing of the past—with very white flesh, chiefly on the breast and back. Then follows the Houdan, with pink legs and very fine flesh; the Game, darker-skinned and small, but with flesh of a fine rich flavour; the Langshan, with dark legs and plenty of flesh, chiefly on the breast; and, last of all, the Brahma, which carries the flesh principally on the thighs. This last-mentioned breed is excellent when young.

Those who have to purchase their poultry when required, as the majority of us have to do, cannot get far wrong in their choice if they study the following indications. Chickens should be chosen with small bones, short legs, and clean, white-looking flesh. Those with white legs are generally considered the best for boiling, and the black-legged ones for roasting. Cocks should have short spurs, smooth legs, and a short, smooth, bright-coloured comb. Hens should be full-breasted and smooth-legged. Capons, when really fine, have a fat vein underneath the wing, a short pale comb, and smooth legs. Ducks should have the breast plump and firm, and the skin clear and fresh-looking. If the breast is lean, and feels soft and flabby to the touch, the bird is either old or stale. A goose, if it is young and fresh, will have a plump breast, white skin, and feet yellow and pliable. If the latter are red, or stiff, it is wise to pass the bird over and go farther before purchasing. In buying a turkey, choose, if possible, a hen. If young the legs will be black and quite smooth, and if perfectly fresh the flesh will be firm, the eyes bright, and the feet supple. The age of a cock turkey can easily be told by the length of its spurs.

The housewife who is willing to give the time and attention necessary to become acquainted with these important details, will be amply repaid when she feels that she can rely implicitly on her own judgment, and is not, therefore, in any way dependent on the opinions of others.

CHAPTER II.

CHICKENS.

Plain boiled—boiled in sauce—fricasseed—with vegetable garnish—curried—with rice border—with macaroni—panada—broth—soup—roast—with stuffing—à la Marengo—à l'Estragon—aux fines herbes—stewed in peas—baked—pie—à la Sainte Menehould—broiled—pounded—cutlets—grilled—fried —fritters—minced—rissoles—pulled—patties—potted—scalloped—sandwiches—mould—galantine—salad.

Chicken, plain boiled.—When the fowl has been properly prepared, wash it quickly in lukewarm water. Truss it firmly and put it into a saucepan with sufficient hot water to entirely cover it. As soon as the water boils, carefully remove the scum, and draw the pan on one side where the contents will only simmer. The great thing to be remembered when boiling a chicken is, that the more slowly and evenly it is cooked, the nicer and tenderer it will be. When done enough, place the fowl on a hot dish, pour over it a little of the sauce, and send the rest to table in a tureen. It is impossible to fix the exact time required for boiling a chicken, as that, of course, must vary according to the size and age of the bird; a very young one would be sufficiently cooked in half an hour, while an old bird—which can be rendered quite as delicious by judicious management—will sometimes require to simmer for two, or even three hours, in order to make it quite tender. The sauces served with boiled chicken are very numerous, but the most popular are parsley and butter, oyster, and white mushroom sauce, recipes for which are given in the chapter on sauces.

Chicken, boiled in sauce.—A chicken cooked in the following manner possesses a much finer flavour than when plain boiled, although the latter is generally considered the most suitable for persons in delicate health. Put four ounces of good beef dripping into a deep frying-pan, and when it is quite hot, fry in it by degrees, six small onions cut in slices, a carrot and two or three outer sticks of celery cut in small pieces, and a teacupful of button mushrooms carefully cleaned. When nicely coloured, drain these from the fat, and put them into a saucepan. Cover them with cold water, or stock, and add a bunch of savoury herbs, a blade of mace, three or four cloves, and a sufficient seasoning of salt and pepper. Simmer all together gently until the sauce is fully flavoured. While this is being done, cut a fine fowl up into neat joints, and sprinkle over each piece a little flour mixed with a seasoning of salt and pepper. When the sauce has simmered long enough, strain it into another saucepan; add the chicken and a glass of claret, and simmer again, very gently, until the chicken is sufficiently cooked, which will be in thirty or forty minutes. If the sauce is not smooth and rather thick, add a small piece of butter rolled in flour. The liver of the fowl, too, may be boiled, pounded, and added to the sauce if desired. Arrange the joints neatly on a hot dish, pour the sauce over, and serve.

Chicken, fricasseed.—Cut up the bird into small neat joints; soak these in cold milk and water for ten minutes, then put them into a saucepan with a bunch of savoury herbs, an onion stuck with four cloves, a teaspoonful of salt, half that quantity of pepper, and sufficient warm water to entirely cover the whole. When the water boils, remove the scum and draw the pan on one side; let the contents simmer very slowly for about half an hour until the meat is quite tender. Place the joints of fowl neatly on a hot dish, pour over and around them some nicely made mushroom sauce, and serve. If fresh mushrooms cannot be conveniently obtained, a very good sauce may be made with mushroom powder.

Chickens with Vegetable Garnish.—Prepare and partially boil the following vegetables :—Two carrots, one turnip, a dozen mushrooms, a dozen tiny onions, a few sticks of celery, and a score of Brussels sprouts. When nearly soft, cut the carrots and turnip first into thin slices, then stamp the slices out in pretty fanciful shapes with a vegetable cutter. Cut half a pound of streaky bacon into small dice; fry these lightly, then put them into a saucepan with the prepared vegetables and a pint of good brown stock. Add the flesh cut from a nice plump fowl, in as large neat pieces as possible, and let all simmer gently for twenty-five minutes. A teaspoonful of salt, half that quantity of white pepper, a little pounded mace, and a glass of white wine may now be added. Simmer for a few minutes longer, then remove the meat, and, if necessary, thicken the gravy with a spoonful of corn-flour mixed to a thin paste with cold water or stock. Strain the gravy over the chicken, and arrange the vegetables round about so as to form a dainty-looking border; first a few mushrooms grouped together, then a few Brussels sprouts, a little of the celery finely chopped, then tiny heaps of the carrots, turnips, onions, and so on. This forms a very tempting-looking dish indeed when nicely done. Garnish the edge of the dish with toasted sippets, and serve very hot. If preferred, the fowl may be cut into joints instead of only the flesh being used. This may, perhaps, appear to some a much more economical proceeding, but, of course, no housewife worthy the name would ever dream of throwing away the bones in the first case as useless ; they could be used for the making of broth, or good white stock, that most valuable item in nearly every sort of delicate, savoury cookery.

Curried Chicken.—Choose a fine plump bird, one with small bones, short legs, and nice clean-looking white flesh ; divide it into neat joints, and fry these for five minutes in boiling dripping or butter. Drain off all the fat carefully, then put the fowl into a saucepan with a tablespoonful of finely minced onion and a stick of celery also cut fine, a dozen button mushrooms, and sufficient good white stock— made from chicken or veal bones—to cover all. Set the saucepan by the side of the fire and let the contents simmer gently for half an hour, then add a tablespoonful of curry paste, and a dessertspoonful of ground rice, mixed to a smooth paste with a little cold water ; simmer a few minutes longer, then arrange the chicken on a hot dish. Add two or three tablespoonfuls of hot cream—the more the better—to the curry, pour it over the fowl, and serve, surrounded with a border of rice properly prepared.

Rice Border.—This is a very popular accompaniment to many other dishes beside chicken, and is to be highly recommended on account of its wholesomeness. The chief point to be attended to in the preparation of the rice is to have every grain separate and distinct; it must be quite soft and tender, and at the same time unbroken. Wash the rice—Carolina is the best—in several waters to insure its being perfectly clean; pick out every grain that is unhusked, or at all discoloured, and put the rest to boil in plenty of water, cold and slightly salted. The great secret of having the rice whole is to be generous in the supply of water; it can never be properly cooked for this purpose in any other way. Let the water come slowly to a boil, then leave the pan lid off and allow the rice to boil gently for about half an hour, by which time it will probably be soft enough. Do not stir the rice while it is cooking, just shake the pan about gently every now and then to prevent it sticking to the bottom. When sufficiently boiled, drain the rice in a strainer or colander, then place it before the fire for a short time to dry; it is then ready to form into a neat firm border round the dish which it is to accompany. Some persons like to have the rice flavoured with salt, curry powder, &c., while others prefer it plain. We may, therefore, leave this point for the housewife herself to decide, as she, of course, knows best the tastes of those for whom she has to cater.

Chicken with Macaroni.—Put half a pound of pipe macaroni into a saucepan with a quart of cold water, and a teaspoonful of salt; let it boil for twenty minutes, then drain off all the water and add a little milk instead. Drop a large onion stuck with three or four cloves in the centre, add a seasoning of salt and pepper, and let all boil gently until the macaroni is quite tender, but not broken. Remove the onion and cloves, as it was only their flavour that was required, and grate over the macaroni four ounces of fine cheese. Parmesan is generally used for this purpose, though some prefer Cheddar. Have ready a fowl trussed and boiled in the usual way; place it on a dish, spread over it the macaroni and cheese, and serve as hot as possible.

Chicken Panada.—This is a dish to be highly recommended for children or persons in delicate health, being very easy to digest, and full of nutriment. Boil a nice plump chicken till quite tender in sufficient water to cover it. Strip off all the meat from the bones, free it from every particle of gristle, and pound it in a mortar until it forms a perfectly smooth paste. Add from time to time, while pounding, a little of the liquid in which the fowl was boiled, a seasoning of salt, nutmeg, and, if approved, a grating of fresh lemon rind. Put this preparation into a saucepan with sufficient of the liquid to make it the consistency of very thick cream, or even a trifle thicker; let it simmer—not boil—for a few minutes, then it is ready to serve. If intended for an invalid the panada should be served accompanied by dainty little sippets of toasted bread; but if for children, some well-cooked vegetables may be eaten with it.

Chicken Broth.—This is another dish suitable for invalids or children, who require quite a different style of cookery from the ordinary. It is always wise for a housewife to acquaint herself thoroughly with the details of invalid cookery, as she is almost sure, at some time or other, to be called upon to practise it. Chicken broth can be, and often is, made from the inferior joints of the fowl only, the finer and more delicate parts having been used to make an entrée; but, of course, if a whole chicken can be afforded, the broth will contain a much larger amount of nourishment, and this is just what an invalid requires—quality, not quantity. Put the fowl, if a good-sized one, into three pints of cold water, with a little salt, but no other seasoning, as these are better added afterwards according to the taste of the invalid. Simmer very gently for three hours, or until all the good is drawn out of the chicken, being careful to remove every particle of fat as it rises to the surface. A little rice, pearl barley, oatmeal, or arrowroot may be boiled in the broth, and will be found a great improvement. Besides making the broth more nutritious, any of these ingredients will absorb a portion of the chicken fat, thus rendering the preparation smoother, and easier to digest. It is best, whenever possible, to make chicken broth, or indeed any other kind of broth or soup, the day before it is required. It can then stand until quite cold, when any fat there may be remaining in it will rise to the top. This will form a stiff cake, which can be easily removed next morning.

Chicken Soup.—This is generally considered a great dainty, altogether a different dish from chicken broth. It is made as follows : Prepare two fine plump birds in the usual manner ; put them into a stew-pan with two quarts of good white stock, nicely flavoured, and freed entirely from all fat and sediment. Add a turnip, a carrot, a few outer sticks of celery cut into good-sized pieces, and let the whole simmer slowly for an hour, counting from the time the liquid came to a boil. Remove the fowls from the pan, cut off all the white meat, and return the rest to the soup, where it may be allowed to simmer for a couple of hours longer. Put four ounces of crumb of stale bread into a basin, pour over it as much boiling milk as it is likely to absorb, and cover the basin closely. When well soaked, drain the bread from any liquid which may remain and put it in a mortar, or large strong basin, with the flesh which was cut from the fowls. Pound these to a smooth paste, then add by degrees the soup when it has been boiled sufficiently, and carefully strained from the vegetables used for flavouring. Season the soup pleasantly with salt, pepper, and a very little powdered mace, or powdered cloves. Press the mixture through a sieve—a process which undoubtedly requires some patience, but which is nevertheless indispensable in the making of good soups—then pour it into a clean saucepan; add a pint of hot milk or cream, let it boil up once more, then serve. If not sufficiently thick, a spoonful of arrowroot, or cornflour, mixed to a thin paste with cold water, may be added.

Roast Chicken.—Young spring chickens are generally roasted without any stuffing, as their flavour is considered sufficiently delicious of itself; but that, of course, is entirely a matter of individual taste. Great care must be taken in preparing the birds, the flesh being so tender that it easily tears. When the inside has been wiped thoroughly clean, put in an ounce of fresh butter, and truss the bird firmly. Cover the breast with well-greased paper, and roast it either before a clear hot fire or in a brisk oven. In either instance it must be basted frequently while cooking. Thirty or thirty-five minutes will be ample time to roast a small bird. Serve it on a bed of fresh crisp watercress.

The same, with stuffing.—If it is thought desirable to have the chicken stuffed, a delightful forcemeat can be made as follows: Chop two ounces of beef suet finely and put it in a basin with two tablespoonfuls of sifted bread crumbs, one tablespoonful of parsley minced very fine, the grated rind of half a fresh lemon, the liver of the bird—previously boiled and chopped small—and salt and pepper to taste. Bind the mixture with a well-beaten egg, then stuff and roast the chicken in the ordinary way.

Chicken à la Marengo.—Divide a good-sized bird into joints, season these with salt and pepper and put them into a deep frying-pan, in which has been melted four ounces of butter, or clarified fat; fry the chicken for a quarter of an hour, then add a small onion roughly minced, and a bunch of sweet herbs; in another quarter of an hour drain the joints very carefully from the fat, &c., and place them on a dish. Set the dish in the oven to keep hot while the sauce is being finished. Mix a tablespoonful of flour with cold water, and add it to the contents of the frying-pan, with as much stock as will make the sauce the consistency of thick cream; stir it over the fire till it looks thick and smooth, then strain it over the chicken. Garnish the dish with fried eggs, or stewed mushrooms, and serve very hot.

Chicken à l'Estragon.—This is a rather more uncommon method of roasting a fowl. Put a handful of tarragon leaves to soak in hot water for five minutes, then dry them, and chop them as fine as possible. Make a forcemeat of the following ingredients: the liver of the bird, boiled and minced small, two ounces of ham or good bacon, the grated rind of a fresh lemon, a little of the chopped tarragon, and a sufficient seasoning of salt and pepper. When thoroughly mixed, stuff the bird with this, truss it in

the usual way, cover the breast with slices of thinly
cut bacon, and roast either before the fire, or in the
oven, whichever is most convenient. Put the remainder of the tarragon leaves into a saucepan with half
a pint of nicely flavoured stock, a little salt and
pepper, a teaspoonful of lemon juice, and an ounce
of butter well kneaded with flour. Stir this sauce
over the fire until it boils, then serve it with the
chicken. If the flavour of tarragon is objected to,
parsley may be used instead.

Chicken aux fines herbes.—Boil and chop
the liver of the bird ; mix it with a teaspoonful each
of parsley, chervil, and tarragon, all finely minced,
and add four pounded cloves, a little powdered
thyme, and a seasoning of pepper and salt. Mix
these ingredients thoroughly and work them well
together with about an ounce of butter. Put this
forcemeat inside the chicken, and secure the opening
of the bird firmly to prevent the stuffing escaping
during the process of cooking. Cover the breast
with either slices of fat bacon, or buttered paper,
and roast in the usual way. The gravy special for
this dish is made as follows: Put four ounces of
butter into a saucepan, and when it melts throw in a
carrot, a large onion, and two sticks of celery, all cut
in small pieces. Fry these for a few minutes, then
add half a pint of good brown stock, a teaspoonful
of arrowroot, mixed with cold water, a teaspoonful
each of the herbs used in the forcemeat, two whole
cloves, half a dozen pepper-corns, half a teaspoonful
of salt, and if liked, a glass of wine. Let these
simmer gently for quite an hour, then strain the
gravy over the chicken, and serve.

Chicken stewed in Peas.—A most delicious
dish for spring. Prepare a nice plump young bird

and cut it into neat joints; put these into a saucepan with a bunch of fresh herbs—a few sprigs of parsley, thyme, and a bay-leaf tied together—an ounce of butter, a little salt and pepper, and a quart of fine fresh green peas—measured, of course, after being shelled. Pour over the whole half a pint of good white stock, cover the pan closely, and let the contents stew just as gently as possible until the chicken is quite tender, and the peas soft without being at all broken. Mix an ounce of butter with a teaspoonful of flour and a few drops of lemon juice; put this into the saucepan and shake it gently about until the peas are nicely coated and the butter entirely melted. Serve the chicken in the centre of a hot dish with the peas forming a border round about. This dish must never be cooked quickly; if allowed to boil, even for a moment, the meat will become hard and tough, the liquid will be exhausted before its time, and the peas, in all probability, will be burnt; thus the whole secret of its being cooked to perfection lies in the fact of its being stewed gently and slowly—a fact which it is sometimes very difficult for young housewives to believe. They are so apt to think that boiling and simmering mean the same thing, while, in reality, there is all the difference in the world.

Baked Chicken.—Cut the fowl into small joints and put them to soak for ten minutes in cold milk and water, mix together on a plate a tablespoonful of flour, a teaspoonful of salt, a saltspoonful of pepper, and a very little pounded mace; dry the joints of chicken slightly and sprinkle them freely with this mixture, pressing it well in; lay a few slices of rather fat bacon at the bottom of a deep-pie dish, place the chicken upon these, and pour over half a pint of good stock, fill up the dish to the top with rice which has been boiled in milk until quite tender, cover the dish with a thick sheet of buttered paper or an old plate, and bake for an hour and a quarter in a moderate oven. If preferred the fowl may be covered with well-mashed potatoes instead of the rice, in which case the top should be prettily marked and nicely browned.

Chicken Pie.—Divide two chickens into joints and put the trimmings, necks, leg bones, &c., into a stew-pan with a little salt, pepper, two or three cloves or a blade of mace, an onion cut in pieces, a bunch of savoury herbs, and a pint of cold water. Let all simmer together for about an hour and a half; this is intended for the gravy. Line the edges of a pie dish with good pastry—suet crust will answer the purpose splendidly if the pie is to be served hot; but if it is to be eaten cold, butter, or a mixture of butter and lard, should be used. Put a layer of the chicken at the bottom of the dish, then a layer of ham cut in small thin slices, next a layer of nicely prepared force-meat, and last of all some hard-boiled eggs cut in quarters. Repeat in this order until the dish is sufficiently full. Moisten with a cupful of water or stock, and put on a cover of the pastry, rolled out about a third of an inch in thickness; wet the edges of the pastry and press them firmly together to make them adhere. Ornament the pie tastefully with the odd pieces of pastry left over, and brush the top—but not the sides—over lightly with beaten egg. Make a small hole in the centre of the top through which the steam can escape, and bake in a well-heated oven. If the crust is in danger of becoming too brown it may be covered with a sheet of buttered paper; and to ascertain when the pie is sufficiently cooked, run a bright skewer, or knitting needle, into the centre ; if it goes through easily the meat is done enough. Before serving the pie the gravy must be strained and poured in through the hole in the top.

Chicken à la Sainte Menehould.—Fricassee a

fowl so that the gravy will form a solid jelly when cold. Put the joints on one side until wanted, then dip them into beaten egg, and cover with fine bread crumbs. Let them lie for a quarter of an hour, then repeat the process. Fry the chicken thus prepared in boiling butter or good beef dripping for about fifteen minutes, turning the joints over when half done. Serve neatly arranged on a very hot dish, covered with a napkin, and accompanied by some good mushrooms, or egg sauce.

Broiled Chicken.—A small bird should always

be chosen for cooking in this fashion, as a large one makes rather an ugly dish. Prepare the bird in the usual way, then cut it right down the back ; truss it as for boiling and flatten each portion as much as possible. Put the chicken into hot water, allow it to come to boiling point, remove the scum, and simmer for ten minutes. When quite cold, brush the pieces over with fine salad oil or clarified butter, and broil them over a clear slow fire. Put the inside of the bird to the fire first, and when half done, turn it. It should be coloured a lovely light brown when finished. Serve very hot, and send bread sauce and rich brown gravy to table with it as accompaniments.

Pounded Chicken.—Roast a fine plump bird,

and while still hot cut it up into joints. Remove the flesh from the breast in as long, neatly-cut slices as possible, and set them aside until required.

Strip all the rest of the meat from the bones, mince it, then put it in a mortar and pound it to a smooth paste. To assist the process of pounding, add, from time to time, a few spoonfuls of stock, and suitable seasonings. Put the preparation into a saucepan with cream enough to moisten it, stir for a few minutes until thoroughly hot, then turn it out into the centre of a hot dish. Fry the slices of fowl taken from the breast in hot butter, just long enough to make them hot through ; arrange them neatly on the top of the mince, and garnish round the edge of the dish with curled bacon, that is, very thinly cut slices of bacon which have been rolled up and fastened with a tiny skewer previous to being fried. A fresh lemon, cut in quarters, should be sent to table with this dish.

Chicken Cutlets.—Take the remains of one or more fowls, either roast or boiled, and cut the flesh into pieces as large and neat-shaped as possible. The cutlets must be even in size and shape or the nice appearance of the dish will be destroyed. Mix together on a plate some salt, pepper, finely minced parsley, and grated cheese ; press this mixture firmly into the meat, first on one side then on the other, and let the cutlets lie for a quarter of an hour. Afterwards dip them in beaten egg, cover with fine bread crumbs, and fry in boiling fat until nicely browned and crisp. Put a mound of well-cooked vegetables in the centre of a hot dish, sorrel, spinach, green peas, or something of that sort, and arrange the cutlets tastefully round about, each one placed on a piece of well-buttered toast, the same size and shape as the cutlet. Some rich brown gravy, made from the bones and trimmings, should be served with this dish.

c

Grilled Chicken.—The legs and wings of the bird are the most suitable parts for this purpose. Remove the skin and score the flesh in several places, rather deeply; rub in either some curry powder, or a hot mixture composed of salt, pepper, cayenne, dry mustard, and butter: This part of the business should always be done on the previous night, or at any rate several hours before the dish is required. Brush the joints over with clarified butter, and grill them over a clear hot fire for ten minutes. If preferred, the chicken may be wrapped in buttered paper before being put on the gridiron, in which case it is safe from being burnt, or blacked, but it loses, in a great measure, the colour and crispness which make this dish look so dainty. Serve dry.

Fried Chicken.—This dish is also made from the remains of cold chicken. Cut what is left into neat pieces, lay these on a plate and sprinkle over them some salt, pepper, and finely minced parsley. Cover them with finest salad oil, and squeeze over them the juice of a large fresh lemon. Let the chicken lie in this marinade for an hour, in order to imbibe the flavour; then drain the pieces, dip them in flour seasoned with salt and pepper, and fry in fat. Sometimes this dish is served dry, on a hot dish, covered with a napkin, and garnished with fried parsley; but if a gravy is preferred, an excellent one can be made as follows: Put a breakfast-cupful of stock into a saucepan with an onion, half-a-dozen cloves, a few sprigs of fresh parsley, half-a-dozen peppercorns, an inch of lemon rind, and some salt. Let these ingredients simmer for an hour, then strain and serve. If thick gravy is preferred, stir in a spoonful of arrowroot, or cornflour, mixed first with a little cold water.

Chicken Fritters.—Take any remains of cold fowl there may be in the house, cut them into neat pieces, and prepare them in the same manner as directed for "chicken cutlets," only substituting grated lemon rind for the cheese. When the chicken is ready, dip each piece in some carefully made frying batter, and fry in plenty of boiling fat until coloured a lovely light brown. Drain away every particle of grease, so as to leave the fritters dry and crisp; pile them nicely on a hot dish, covered with a napkin or dish paper, and intersperse tiny sprigs of fried parsley here and there. Serve as hot and as soon after being cooked as possible. To make the frying batter, mix three tablespoonfuls of flour to the proper consistency with lukewarm water; add a good pinch of salt, and two tablespoonfuls of finest salad oil. Let the batter stand for several hours—overnight in cold weather—then, just before using, throw in the whites of two eggs beaten to a stiff froth. To fry parsley proceed as follows : Wash the parsley thoroughly, and dry it by tossing it to and fro in a clean cloth; throw it into boiling fat and let it remain until quite crisp—not a moment longer or it will be spoilt—remove it from the pan with a slice, and lay it on blotting paper to drain. It does not require more than a few moments to fry.

Minced Chicken.—No matter how small the pieces, let them all be gathered together. Free the meat from all skin, gristle, and bones, and mince it very finely. Put half a pint of good white stock into a saucepan, thicken it slightly with arrowroot, and let it come to boiling point. Add a dozen mushrooms chopped small, a teacupful of cream, or good milk, salt, and pepper, a dessertspoonful of minced parsley, a teaspoonful of grated lemon rind, and the minced chicken. Simmer gently for a quarter of an hour, then turn the mince out on to a hot dish, garnish round the edge with croutons, and serve hot. Croutons are simply slices of stale bread stamped out in pretty fanciful shapes, and fried in boiling fat until crisp and brown. They are generally preferred to toasted bread.

Chicken Rissoles.—When the meat has been finely minced as in the above recipe, supposing there is half a pound of it, mix it with three ounces of minced ham, three heaped tablespoonfuls of sifted bread crumbs, an ounce of fresh butter, a teaspoonful of grated lemon rind, a saltspoonful of salt, and a pinch of pepper. Mix these ingredients thoroughly and moisten the preparation with a little stock in which sufficient gelatine has been melted to make it form a jelly when cold. Allow the mixture to become quite cold, then divide it into small portions; roll these up into tiny balls, enclose each one in good pastry rolled out very thin, and fry them in boiling fat until lightly coloured. Drain off all the fat, and serve the rissoles piled on a napkin; garnish the dish prettily with fried parsley.

Pulled Chicken.—Roast a chicken in the usua way, and when cold cut off the legs, sidesmen, and back, and sprinkle over them some salt, pepper, and pounded mace. Dip them in beaten egg, cover with bread crumbs, and set them on one side until required. Remove the skin from the breast and wings, and pull off what is known as the "white meat" in long thin flakes. Put these into a saucepan with some good white stock, pleasantly flavoured; let the meat get hot through without boiling, then turn it out on a hot dish. Broil the legs, back, and sidesmen, and arrange them neatly on the top; have ready some small forcemeat balls which have been fried in hot fat and carefully drained. Place these round the edge of the dish, and just before serving squeeze over all a few drops of lemon juice.

Chicken Patties.—When only a very small proportion of chicken remains, this is an excellent method of using it up. Free the meat from skin, bones, and gristle, mince it finely, then weigh it and mix with it half its weight in cold cooked ham, also minced. Supposing there are ten ounces of meat altogether, add two ounces of butter well kneaded with flour, a small teacupful of milk, the same of good strong stock, a sufficient seasoning of pepper and salt, the grated rind of a small lemon, a dessertspoonful of finely chopped parsley, and a few mushrooms chopped small, or a little of the powder. Put all these ingredients into a saucepan and stir them over the fire for about ten minutes; the preparation needs to be made thoroughly hot, but it must not be allowed to boil. Turn it out on to a plate to get quite cold before using. Line-out some small patty tins with good short pastry rolled out very thin; three parts fill them with the mince, and cover with a lid of the pastry. Moisten the edges and press them firmly together to make them adhere; mark them prettily round about, make a tiny hole in the centre, and brush the tops over very lightly with beaten egg. Bake in a brisk oven for ten or fifteen minutes.

Potted Chicken.—A little of this delicacy, spread on slices of thin bread and butter, forms a most delicious breakfast relish. Roast a chicken, and when cold strip off every particle of flesh from the bones, free it entirely from skin and gristle, then weigh it, and to every pound allow four ounces of ham and four ounces of butter. Put the whole into a mortar and pound them to a perfectly smooth paste, adding during the process sufficient salt, pepper, cayenne, pounded mace, and grated nutmeg, to season rather highly. Press the mixture when finished into small jars, cover the tops with a layer of clarified butter a quarter of an inch thick, store in a cool dry place, and use when required.

Scalloped Chicken.—When the meat has been finely minced put it into a saucepan with a teacupful of stock, or milk which has been slightly thickened with a spoonful of cornflour; season pleasantly with salt, cayenne, and pounded mace, and stir over the fire till the mince is thoroughly heated. Have ready some scallop shells, butter them liberally, and sprinkle over each a thick layer of fine bread crumbs. Fill them with the mince, and sprinkle more crumbs on the top. Put a tiny piece of butter on each, and bake in a hot oven until nicely browned. Arrange the shells neatly on a folded napkin, and garnish the dish with fried parsley.

Chicken and Ham Sandwiches.—When nicely prepared these form a very superior breakfast or luncheon dish. Make a savoury mince of cold chicken and cold boiled ham, two-thirds of the former to one-third of the latter; season rather highly, and moisten with milk or white stock. Put the preparation into a saucepan by the side of the fire and allow it to simmer very gently for ten minutes. Meantime cut some slices of stale bread a quarter of an inch thick, stamp these out in small rounds or squares, and fry them in butter till lightly browned.

Put them together in twos with a layer of the mince between; press them firmly together, and place them side by side on a baking sheet. Grate some good cheese thickly over the top, and bake in a quick oven for a few minutes. Serve on a napkin, and as hot as possible.

Chicken Mould.—Boil three tablespoonfuls of the best Carolina rice in a pint of nicely flavoured white stock until the liquid is all absorbed and the rice swollen out to the full. Turn it out into a large basin and add to it two well-beaten eggs, a few spoonfuls of milk, and three-quarters of a pound of chicken and ham minced together. Season with salt, white pepper, and pounded mace. Stir briskly for a few minutes to thoroughly incorporate all the ingredients, then turn the mixture into a well-buttered mould; cover the top with a sheet of buttered paper, and bake in a moderate oven for an hour. Turn the pudding out carefully on the centre of a hot dish, and pour some nicely stewed mushrooms round about.

Galantine of Chicken.—Bone a large chicken and lay it flat on the table, skin downwards. Season with salt, cayenne, and aromatic spices; then spread over it a layer of good sausage-meat, some thin slices of tongue, ham, and hard-boiled eggs. Repeat the process until the galantine is sufficiently full, then sew it up firmly with twine; roll it in a buttered cloth, fasten the ends securely and braize it in veal stock for two hours. Let it remain in the stock till nearly cold, then take it up and place it between two dishes; put a heavy weight on the top, and let it remain untouched till next day. When the twine and cloth have been removed, place the galantine on a dish, give it one or two coats of glaze, and ornament it tastefully with aspic jelly. Before serving garnish the edge of the dish with a border of finely-shred lettuce and hard-boiled eggs cut in slices. This forms a delightful supper dish.

Chicken Salad.—Boil a fine plump chicken until tender, and when cold cut off the meat in small, neat pieces. Have ready in a salad bowl some carefully-prepared spring salad ; lettuces, radishes, water-cress, small cress, endive, celery, and spring onions are all suitable. Each separate ingredient requires to be washed and made thoroughly dry previous to being chopped. Arrange the pieces of chicken neatly on the top of the salad, and pour over all some mayonnaise sauce. Ornament the top prettily with boiled beetroot, stamped out in pretty shapes, and chopped aspic jelly. For the making of mayonnaise sauce, see chapter on sauces.

CHAPTER III.

DUCKS.

À la Française—à l'Italienne—à la mode—à l'Indienne—
German fashion—stewed with olives—salmi—boiled—pie—
roast—hashed—stewed—savoury—rolled—braised with vegetables — filleted — broiled — soup—steamed — ragoût — wild—
cooked in sauce—devilled.

Duck à la Française.—Put a pint of good beef
stock or gravy into a saucepan, with a breakfast-
cupful of chestnuts previously roasted and peeled; two
medium-sized onions, sliced thin and fried in butter;
a teaspoonful of powdered sage and thyme, mixed
with pepper and salt to taste. Lard the breast of
the duck with fat bacon, and roast it either before
the fire or in a hot oven for twenty minutes, then
put it into the saucepan with the gravy, &c. Let it
stew gently for half an hour longer, then put it on
a dish and place it in the oven to keep hot. Thicken
the gravy with an ounce of butter well kneaded with
flour, and add a glass of port wine. Stir for a few
minutes until the gravy boils up briskly, then pour
it over the duck and serve.

Duck à l'Italienne.—Prepare a duck as if for
roasting, and put it into a saucepan just large enough
to hold it. The pan must first be lined out with thin
slices of fat bacon sprinkled over with chopped par-

sley, chives, thyme, and lemon rind. Cover the duck
with stock or water—the former, of course, to be preferred—add a carrot cut in pieces, an onion stuck
with half-a-dozen cloves, a glass of wine, and a seasoning of salt and pepper—very little of the former,
as the bacon will supply nearly all that is required.
Baste frequently and cook gently until done enough,
the length of time, of course, being regulated according to the size of the duck. Meantime prepare the
following sauce:—Put two ounces of butter into a
small saucepan, and when it melts work in smoothly,
with a wooden spoon, a tablespoonful of flour. When
this is done, add a breakfast-cupful of good brown
gravy or stock, a dessert-spoonful of finely-chopped
parsley, the same quantity of onion finely minced, a
dozen mushrooms also chopped fine, half a teaspoonful of salt, and a pinch of cayenne. Boil the sauce
very gently for ten minutes, then pour it over the
duck and serve very hot. The sauce should be rather
thick and a nice rich brown in colour; if not sufficiently dark, add a few drops of browning.

Duck à la mode.—Cut a nice large duck into
neat joints, sprinkle these with flour which has been
seasoned with salt, pepper, and a grated lemon rind,
and fry them in a saucepan with plenty of boiling
butter until they are lightly browned. Drain away
all the fat, and cover the duck with half a pint of
gravy and a little port wine. Add a bunch of herbs,
two small onions minced very fine, a pinch of cayenne,
a dessert-spoonful of ketchup, and a teaspoonful of
cornflour mixed to a smooth paste with a little water.
Cover the pan very closely, and allow the duck to
simmer for half an hour, when it will be done enough.
Have ready a hot dish upon which has been placed a
ring of mashed potatoes, arrange the joints of the

duck neatly in the centre, remove the bunch of herbs
and pour the sauce over the duck, but not over the
potato border. This latter should have a few sprigs
of crisp parsley inserted here and there. When nicely
prepared, this dish is an exceedingly dainty one,
pleasing alike to the eye and the palate.

Duck à l'Indienne.—This is a most convenient
method of using up the remaining parts of a roast
duck after the fillets have been served às an entrée.
Put a dessert-spoonful of curry paste, a dessert-spoonful of curry powder, and a teaspoonful of cornflour
into a basin; mix these to a smooth paste with a little
water or stock, and add slowly a pint of boiling
stock, stirring all the time. Pour this sauce into a
very clean saucepan, and stir over the fire till it
becomes thick and smooth, then lay in the joints of
the duck and simmer gently until quite hot through;
they will take about half an hour. Arrange the
pieces neatly on a hot dish and strain the sauce over.
Garnish with sliced tomatoes and cut lemon.

Duck, German Fashion.—In Germany the
birds are prepared and trussed in the same manner
as they are done here, but the stuffing is altogether
different. Soak six ounces of stale bread in cold
water for ten minutes, then press it out and mix it
with two ounces of warm butter, two well-beaten
eggs, a finely-minced onion, salt, pepper, and a little
grated nutmeg. Parboil the liver of the duck, chop
it very small, and add it to the other ingredients.
Another way is to peel, core, and chop small as many
good baking apples as will fill the bird; mix these
with two ounces of currants well cleaned and rinsed
in boiling water, and two ounces of fresh butter.
While a third method is to fill the duck with chest-

nut stuffing, prepared pretty much in the same way as we make it here for the stuffing of turkeys.

Duck Stewed with Olives.—Prepare the bird in the usual way, and truss it as for boiling. Put it into a stew-pan, the bottom of which has been well covered with slices of rather fat bacon, and add some parsley, thyme, chives, lemon rind, an onion stuck with half-a-dozen cloves, a carrot cut into small pieces, salt, half-a-dozen peppercorns, and sufficient stock or water to cover the duck. Baste frequently, and simmer gently for an hour. Have ready in another saucepan some good brown gravy made in the usual way; put the duck into this, after being braised as directed, add plenty of mushrooms, and some olives which have been soaked for three or four hours, and had the stones removed, and let all simmer slowly for half an hour. Serve the duck on a hot dish, with the sauce poured over. This is a favourite French dish, and will prove an excellent way of cooking an old bird.

Salmi of Duck.—This is a very favourite dish with French epicures as well as English ones. Take the giblets of the duck and put them into a stew-pan with some stock, rather highly seasoned with salt, pepper, and cayenne, an onion cut into small pieces, and half-a-dozen cloves. Put the stew-pan by the side of the fire where the contents can simmer slowly. Roast the duck for about twenty minutes, then cut it up into neat joints. Lay these in the gravy, and allow them to simmer gently for half an hour. Arrange the duck, when done enough, on a hot dish, add the juice of a fresh lemon to the gravy, and strain it carefully over the duck. Serve hot, accompanied by some well-cooked seasonable vegetables.

Boiled Duck.—This is a very highly esteemed dish in some parts of North Wales, so it is quite evident that the originator of the old proverb, "a duck boiled is a duck spoiled," was not a Welshman. The duck must be well salted, then boiled in the same manner as a fowl. When done enough serve it on a hot dish, covered or "smothered" with onion sauce.

Duck Pie.—Prepare a duck in the usual way, and partially roast or boil it; cut it up into small neat joints, and put a layer of these at the bottom of a pie dish. Sprinkle over this a layer of finely-chopped parboiled onions, seasoned with salt, pepper, and powdered sage, then, if liked, a layer of minced apples sweetened to taste. Repeat in this manner until the dish is sufficiently full ; pour over a teacupful of stock, and cover in the usual way with good short pastry. Ornament the top prettily, and make a hole in the centre, through which the steam may escape. Brush the top over lightly with beaten egg, and bake the pie in a brisk oven. Put the giblets, with the neck and the wings, into a saucepan with two ounces of butter, a bunch of herbs, an onion sliced thin, four cloves, half-a-dozen peppercorns, a blade of mace, and an inch of lemon rind. When these have stewed for a few minutes, add two-thirds of a pint of water, put on the pan lid, and let all simmer gently for an hour. When the pie is done enough, strain the gravy, and pour it through the hole in the top.

Roast Duck.—This dish is such a universal favourite, and is so well known, that it requires no recommendation of mine. Two small ducks make a much nicer-looking dish than one very large one; the large ones, as a rule, being rather hard-fleshed, are much more suitable for braising, &c., than roasting. If the poulterer does not prepare the birds, proceed to do so in the following manner: Pluck, singe, and empty them; scald and skin the feet, and twist them round on to the back of the bird; then cut off the head, neck, and pinions, the latter at the first joint, and skewer the ducks firmly, giving to the breast as plump and full an appearance as possible. For the stuffing take half a pound of parboiled onions, chop them very fine, and mix with them three tablespoonfuls of sifted bread crumbs, a dessertspoonful of powdered sage, the liver of the bird parboiled and chopped fine, with salt and pepper to taste. The quantities here given are for one duck; more seasoning can of course be added if thought desirable, but the above mixture will prove a most dainty yet delicate compound, not likely to disagree with anyone. After the duck is stuffed, secure the openings firmly, rub the bird all over with butter, and roast before a clear hot fire, or in a brisk oven. Baste frequently, and when about half done, dredge a little flour over, to give the bird a frothy look. Good-sized ducks require from three-quarters of an hour to an hour for cooking thoroughly; smaller ones from thirty to thirty-five minutes. Serve with good brown gravy and apple sauce.

Hashed Duck.—Take any remains of cold duck there may be, and cut them into as neat pieces as possible. Lay them in a saucepan and sprinkle over them a seasoning of salt, a pinch of cayenne, an onion cut into small pieces, four cloves, and a teaspoonful of chopped lemon rind. Pour over some good stock or gravy, and let all simmer gently together by the side of the fire for half or three-quarters of an hour. Serve in the same manner as "duck à la mode."

Stewed Duck.—The flavour of the bird will be greatly improved if it is roasted for about twenty minutes before being put to stew. A large duck may be used with advantage for this dish. The bird must be well seasoned, both inside and outside, with salt and pepper, be roasted for twenty minutes, then put into a deep saucepan with sufficient good brown stock to entirely cover it; add a large onion, previously sliced and fried in butter, some sage leaves and thyme, a few sprigs of parsley, with salt and pepper to season pleasantly. Cover the pan and let the contents simmer for half an hour, or longer if the bird is not quite tender by that time. Place a large flat bed of well-cooked cabbage or mashed turnips on a hot dish; lay the duck upon this, and when the gravy has been strained, and thickened with a little brown thickening, pour it over all, and serve hot.

Savoury Duck.—Remove the rind from half a pound of streaky bacon and cut it into inch pieces; fry these in a saucepan with an ounce of butter for five minutes, then dredge in very gradually a tablespoonful of flour. After stirring for a few minutes longer add a pint of good brown stock, an onion stuck with half-a-dozen cloves, a bunch of sweet herbs, a teaspoonful of salt, and half that quantity of pepper. Cut up the duck into neat joints, fry these for ten minutes in hot butter, then lay them into the saucepan with the other ingredients. Cover the pan closely, and stew the duck very gently for an

hour, or an hour and a half, until the flesh feels
quite tender when pierced by a skewer. Put a
mound of green peas in the centre of the dish, place
the joints of the duck round about, and strain the
gravy over all. This is one of the best methods of
cooking an old bird, which might prove tough and
comparatively tasteless if roasted, but which can in
this way be rendered as deliciously tender as a
young one.

Rolled Duck.—Bone a duck very carefully so as
not in any way to injure the skin; cut it down the
back, lay it flat upon the table, skin downwards, and
spread over it a thick layer of rich forcemeat, made
as follows :—Half a pound of lean veal, half a
pound of beef suet—both finely minced—a teacupful
of sifted bread crumbs, a tablespoonful of chopped
parsley, the same of minced onion, with a sufficient
seasoning of salt and pepper. Put these ingredients
into a basin, and mix them to a stiff paste with two
well-beaten eggs, and, if necessary, a little milk or
cream. Roll the duck up as firmly and neatly as
possible; secure it with string or narrow tape, and
wrap it in a buttered paper. Lay it in a baking tin
in which has been melted four ounces of good beef
dripping, and bake it in a well-heated oven for an
hour, basting it frequently during the time. A
quarter of an hour before the duck is sufficiently
cooked remove the paper, in order that the bird may
get nicely browned. Serve it with a little good
brown gravy poured over, and send more to table in
a tureen.

Braised Duck, with vegetables.—Choose a
fine young bird, truss it as for roasting, and put it
into a saucepan with three ounces of butter, pepper,

and salt, and a savoury bouquet, *i.e.* some parsley, thyme, marjoram, and a bay-leaf tied together. Set the pan on the fire and fry gently until the duck is nicely browned all over; to accomplish this end the bird must be turned and basted very frequently. Shake in by slow degrees two tablespoonfuls of flour, which must be mixed smoothly with the butter, then add as much stock, or water, as will cover the duck. As soon as the liquid boils draw the saucepan on one side and let it simmer slowly for about an hour, carefully removing the scum as it rises. Have ready some carrots and turnips, cut in slices, then stamped out in pretty fanciful shapes with a cutter, and drop these gently into the saucepan with the duck. When sufficiently cooked, take out the duck first, place it in the centre of a hot dish, then carefully drain the vegetables and arrange them tastefully round about. Thicken the sauce if necessary, then strain it over the duck and serve.

Filleted Duck.—This dish, when nicely prepared, forms as pretty and dainty-looking an entrée as one need wish to see. Roast a fine plump bird in the usual way, but without stuffing, for half an hour; then cut the meat from the breast in long, neat slices, and lay them in a saucepan with a few spoonfuls of rich brown gravy, highly seasoned, and a glass of port; let all simmer gently for a quarter of an hour, then serve the fillets neatly arranged on a border of mashed potatoes. Fill up the centre of the dish with a mound of green peas, and pour the gravy over the duck. Serve very hot.

Broiled Duck.—Divide a duck down the back and flatten both sides as much as possible; truss the legs and wings as for roasting, and prick the flesh

D

all over with a skewer. Make a hot mixture with mustard, pepper, salt, cayenne, and curry powder; rub this thoroughly into the meat, then broil the bird over a clear but rather slow fire, putting the inside to the fire first. The gravy for this dish is made as follows:—Put three tablespoonfuls of rich brown gravy into a stew-pan with an equal quantity of white wine, two tablespoonfuls of ketchup, one of lemon-juice, and one of sugar. Place the duck, when done enough, on a hot dish, outside uppermost, and when the gravy boils, pour it over, and serve. If liked better, the gravy may be slightly thickened with a little brown thickening. (For thickening, see Chap. VII.)

Giblet Soup.—As duck giblets are small, three sets will be required to make a sufficient quantity of soup for six or eight persons. Scald and clean the giblets carefully, then cut them into pieces about an inch long and put them into a saucepan with two quarts of water, a pound of gravy beef cut in pieces, or a good beef bone, which will do quite as well, a large onion cut in quarters, a bunch of herbs, and the rind of a fresh lemon. Simmer gently until the bones are quite loose and the gizzards soft. Now strain the soup into another saucepan and season it pleasantly with salt, pepper, and a pinch of cayenne. The giblets, and beef—if any has been used—must be put in the soup-tureen and kept hot by the fire. Fry some onions, which have been sliced very thin, in hot butter until nicely browned, stir into them a heaped tablespoonful of flour, then add them to the soup and stir until it boils. If not sufficiently thick, a little more flour may be added. Skim off any fat which may rise to the surface, and strain the soup over the giblets in the tureen; add a glass of Madeira, two tablespoonfuls of ketchup, and one of lemon-juice. Serve hot, accompanied by toasted bread cut into dice.

Steamed Duck.—When the bird has been properly prepared and trussed, roast it for twenty minutes, either before a clear fire or in a brisk oven, then lay it in a saucepan upon a bed of vegetables, composed of sliced carrot, turnip, and onion; two sticks of celery cut into small pieces, half-a-dozen cloves, two bay-leaves, a few sage-leaves, and a little stock or water, just sufficient to cover the vegetables. Put on the pan lid and let all stew gently until the vegetables are cooked enough. Probably a little more liquid may have to be added, as the vegetables must not on any account be allowed to burn. When done enough, take up the duck—which ought to have been lying breast uppermost—place it on a hot dish and put it in the oven to keep hot. Press the vegetables patiently through a sieve, and mix the pulp with any liquid which remains in the saucepan, or with a spoonful or two of good gravy. Pour this *purée* round the duck —not over—and serve,

Ragoût of Duck.—This is a very convenient method of using up the remains of cold duck. Chop two medium-sized onions rather fine and fry them in hot fat until they are soft and yellow, then dredge in a little flour, about a tablespoonful, and stir until it, and the onions, are nicely browned, but not at all burnt. Now add half a pint of good stock, salt, pepper, a teaspoonful of tarragon vinegar, and a glass of white wine. Cut the remains of the duck into neat little slices or pieces, lay them into the gravy, and let all simmer, or steam very gently until the meat is thoroughly hot. Put a border of boiled rice, or mashed potatoes, round the edge.

of a hot dish, pour the ragoût into the centre, and serve.

Wild Duck.—The points most to be observed in roasting a wild duck are, first, to retain the gravy well in the breast of the bird, and, secondly, not to lose the delicate flavour through over-dressing. Pluck and draw the bird very carefully, wipe the inside thoroughly clean with a cloth, then scald the feet, and truss the bird in the usual way. Baste it well with butter while it is roasting, and when half done dredge a little flour over to give a nice frothy appearance. Serve with a little good gravy in the dish, and have more sent to table in a tureen. As these birds are small two are generally allowed for a dish.

The same, cooked in Sauce.—Put a pint of good brown stock into a saucepan with a tablespoonful of lemon-juice, a glass of claret, a saltspoonful of mixed spice, the same of white pepper, half a teaspoonful of salt, and an onion stuck with four cloves. Add two tablespoonfuls of sifted bread crumbs, and set the pan on the fire. Cut up the duck into small neat joints, and as soon as the sauce boils put these in, and allow them to simmer for three-quarters of an hour. Arrange the duck neatly on a hot dish, remove the onion, and pour the sauce over the duck. Garnish the dish with sippets of toasted bread.

Devilled Duck.—The legs and wings of a cold roast duck are the most suitable joints for this dish. Rub them entirely over with hot butter, then cover them with a thick layer of devil paste; roll each piece in browned crumbs, place them side by side on a greased baking tin, and bake in a moderate oven.

for twenty minutes. Pile some nicely prepared salad high in the centre of a dish, and when the pieces of duck are quite cold arrange them tastefully round the edge. The devil paste is a most convenient thing for a housewife to keep by her, it can be used in such a variety of ways The ingredients are:—a dessert-spoonful of ordinary mustard, a tablespoonful of French mustard, a tablespoonful of tarragon vinegar, a saltspoonful of salt, and half that quantity of pepper. Mix these thoroughly and put the paste into a jar, cover the top securely, and store in a dry cool place until required.

CHAPTER IV.

GEESE.

Roast—green—à la daube—glazed—à l'Arlesienne—braised —in batter—hashed—grilled—soup—marinaded—pie—Christ-mas pie—boiled—in jelly.

Roast Goose.—When the bird has been plucked, carefully remove the quill-sockets, and singe off the hairs. Cut off the neck quite close to the back, but leave the skin long enough to turn nicely over. After being drawn, wipe the goose thoroughly clean, inside and outside, with a clean cloth; cut off the feet and the pinions at the first joint, pull out the throat, and beat the breast-bone flat with a rolling-pin. Draw the legs up closely and skewer them firmly to the body; the pinions, too, must be dealt with in a similar fashion. Fill with whatever kind of stuffing is being used, secure the openings care-fully, and roast either in a brisk oven or before a bright hot fire, basting frequently. Sage and onion stuffing is generally used, though apple, chestnut, and potato stuffing are all suitable. Serve with good brown gravy and apple sauce, and garnish the dish with sliced lemon.

Green Goose.—Truss the bird in the same manner as a full-grown one, but do not stuff it. When it has been wiped quite clean with a damp cloth, season the inside well with salt and pepper, and put in about three ounces of fresh butter. Roast rather quickly, and when sufficiently done, serve the bird on a hot dish, garnished with watercresses. Good brown gravy should be sent to table with it, also gooseberry, sorrel, or tomato sauce.

Goose à la daube.—An old goose can, with advantage, be cooked in the following manner: Truss the bird as for boiling, cover it with slices of rather fat bacon, and lay it in a saucepan. Add an onion, a carrot cut in pieces, a bunch of savoury herbs, half a dozen peppercorns, a blade of mace, and as much stock or water as will barely cover the goose. Sherry wine and a little brandy are sometimes added, but that, of course, is quite optional. Cover the pan closely, and stew the contents slowly for about four hours. Place the goose on a hot dish, and strain the sauce very carefully over it. Serve very hot.

Glazed Goose.—This dish is cooked in precisely the same manner as the above, only instead of straining the sauce over the goose at once it must be boiled down till it is strong enough to form a jelly when cold. If there is any fear of its not doing this, a little of the bought glaze may be melted down in the usual way and used instead. Brush the goose over with it once or twice, so as to give a clear, bright appearance, letting each coating get dry before adding the next. This forms a very nice supper dish when prettily garnished with fresh parsley, sliced beetroot, and lemons cut in quarters.

Goose à l'Arlesienne.—Prepare and truss a goose in the usual way, and stuff it with forcemeat made as follows: Parboil four large onions, then drain, and chop them quite small; mix with them four table-spoonfuls of sifted bread crumbs, three ounces of fresh butter, a tablespoonful of chopped parsley, pepper, salt, and grated nutmeg, and a dozen chest-nuts which have been blanched like almonds, boiled in stock until quite soft, then chopped finely. When the goose is stuffed and the openings securely fas-tened, put it into a saucepan with a large carrot cut in pieces, a few outer sticks of celery, a bunch of savoury herbs, an onion stuck with half a dozen cloves, a few sprigs of parsley, a blade of mace, a dozen peppercorns, and sufficient stock to cover the bird. Put on the pan lid and stew the goose very gently until quite tender; the length of time re-quired will, of course, be in accordance with the size and age of the bird. When done enough, place the goose on a dish and set it in the oven to keep hot. Strain the liquor into another saucepan; skim off all the fat and let it boil hard for a few minutes, then mix about half a pint of it with an equal quan-tity of tomato pulp or sauce. Pour this over and round the goose, and garnish the dish with baked tomatoes.

Braised Goose with Vegetables.—Cook the goose according to the directions given for "Goose à la daube," using water instead of stock. When sufficiently stewed remove the bird into another saucepan, pour over it a pint of good stock, and add any quantity of mixed vegetables which have been cooked previously; turnips and carrots stamped out in pretty shapes, sprigs of cauliflower, French beans, green peas, any or all of these are suitable. Place the goose—after simmering for a quarter of an hour—upon a hot dish, thicken the sauce slightly with a little brown thickening (see Chap. VII.), and let it boil up; pour it, with the vegetables, over the goose and serve.

Goose in Batter.—When only a very small portion of goose remains, and it is desirable that we should make the most of it, the following recipe will be found excellent:—Strip all the flesh from the bones and cut it into small, neat pieces about an inch long, and half an inch across, and not more than a quarter of an inch thick. Sprinkle these over with salt, pepper, and finely powdered sage, and set them on one side. Make some nice light batter with four tablespoonfuls of flour, half a teaspoonful of salt, two well-beaten eggs, and a little milk. Beat the mixture thoroughly until there are no lumps, then set it in a cool place for a few hours; indeed, it would be all the richer if made the previous night, that is in suitable weather, of course. Beat it again for a minute or two just before using, and pour a little of it at the bottom of a pie dish; next put a layer of the goose, distributing the pieces as evenly as possible, then more batter, and so on until the dish is sufficiently full, letting batter form the topmost layer. Bake in a well-heated oven from half an hour to an hour, according to the size of the dish. It may either be served in the dish in which it has been cooked, or it may be carefully turned out on to a hot dish and garnished with a little fried parsley. The batter should be a trifle thicker than cream, and if nicely cooked will present a very dainty appearance, being well browned all over.

Hashed Goose.—Cut the remains of cold goose into small, neat slices and cover them over till wanted. Chop two medium-sized onions and fry them in a saucepan with an ounce of butter till they are lightly browned, then add as much stock or water as will make sufficient gravy for the hash, the bones and trimmings of the goose, a bunch of herbs, a few sage leaves, salt and pepper to taste, and, if liked, a glass of port or claret. Boil gently until the gravy is rich and good, then strain it into another saucepan, thicken it if necessary, and lay in the pieces of goose. Allow these to get thoroughly hot, but the gravy must not boil after the goose is added. Preserve any stuffing there may be left, and make it hot in the oven. Arrange the goose neatly on a hot dish, pour the gravy over, and garnish with small pieces of toast; place a tiny piece of stuffing on each piece, and serve very hot.

Grilled Goose.—This is a very convenient method of using up the more inferior parts of the bird: the legs, back, rump, and gizzard being the most suitable parts for this dish. Score the flesh in several places and rub in a mixture of salt and pepper, dip each piece in clarified butter, cover with sifted bread crumbs, and broil over a clear hot fire until brightly browned. Arrange the goose tastefully upon a bed of mashed potatoes, garnish the dish with parsley, and serve either dry or accompanied by apple sauce and brown gravy.

Goose Soup.—When a goose has been boiled in stock, excellent soup can be made of the liquid afterwards. Clean and properly prepare the giblets, and put them into the saucepan with the stock; add an onion, a carrot, half a head of celery, and half a und of lean ham; simmer for two hours, then move the giblets into the tureen, strain the soup nd thicken it if desired; season with a pinch of enne and very little salt, add a little sherry or

Madeira, and pour it over the giblets. Serve with toasted bread cut into dice.

Marinaded Goose.—Pluck, singe, and bone a goose. This latter operation can soon be done quite easily with a little practice, but, should some find it too difficult, it may be dispensed with. Stuff the bird with a well-made sage and onion stuffing, highly seasoned, truss it securely, and roast it very quickly for twenty minutes until nicely browned all over. Put it in a saucepan with just sufficient good stock to cover it, and allow it to simmer gently for two hours or more, according to the size and age of the bird, then place it on a dish and put it to keep hot in the oven. Remove all the fat from the gravy, thicken it with an ounce of butter well kneaded with flour, and colour it with a little browning; add a seasoning of salt and pepper, a pounded anchovy, a little grated nutmeg, a tablespoonful of lemon pickle, and a glass of port. Let these simmer for a few minutes, then pour the gravy over the goose and serve.

Goose Pie.—This can either be made with one good-sized goose, or with what is considered better still, two green geese. Put the birds, when properly prepared, into a saucepan with the usual flavouring vegetables and stock or water; stew, or braise very gently till the geese are tender, then cut them into small neat joints. Season the meat with salt and pepper, and put a single layer at the bottom of a pie dish; sprinkle next a layer of finely minced onions, powdered sage, and grated lemon rind; then another layer of meat, and so on until the dish is sufficiently full; pour over the whole half a pint of good brown gravy, pleasantly flavoured, cover with a good short crust, and bake in the usual way.

Christmas Pie.—This is a very old-fashioned dish, which we have often heard of, but seldom seen. It is made by boning a goose, a turkey, a fowl, and a pigeon ; put the turkey inside the goose, the fowl inside the turkey, and the pigeon inside the fowl. The goose thus stuffed may either be baked in a raised crust or in a pie-dish in the ordinary way ; in either case the vacancies must be filled up with good forcemeat, ham, and tongue. When the lid of pastry is put on brush it over with beaten egg, and bake in a well-heated oven from three to four hours. Pour about half a pint of gravy into the pie before baking, and add a little more before sending to table.

Boiled Goose.—Pluck and singe the goose carefully, and lay it to soak in milk and water (lukewarm) for a few hours. Truss and stuff it securely, then put it into a saucepan with sufficient water or stock to cover it. Bring it to a boil, and let it simmer slowly until done enough. Place the bird on a hot dish, pour over it some rich white sauce, and send onion sauce to table as an accompaniment. If stock has been used for boiling the goose in, preserve it to make goose soup with.

Goose in Jelly.—Put the goose, when properly prepared, into a deep pan, and cover it with second stock or water. Add a dessert-spoonful of salt, a teaspoonful of pepper, two onions cut in pieces, two bay leaves, some sprigs of thyme, sage, and parsley, and the rind of a fresh lemon. Simmer all together very gently, until the flesh will leave the bones quite easily; then remove the goose and drain it from the gravy. Take out the bones, which may be returned to the saucepan, and cut the meat into convenient-sized pieces. Taste the gravy and add more seasoning if necessary; after removing the fat, strain the liquid through a jelly bag, or a piece of coarse muslin, and mix with it an ounce of gelatine which has been dissolved in water. Pour a little of this jelly at the bottom of a damp mould and allow it to set, then arrange some pretty devices of cold boiled beetroot, hard-boiled eggs, sprigs of fresh green parsley, and pickles. Pour a little more jelly over these, and when it stiffens put in the pieces of meat, not too closely, as room must be left for the jelly to flow freely between. Set the mould in a cool place and let it remain till next day, then turn it carefully out, garnish with parsley, sliced lemon, and boiled beetroot, and serve. Any kind of poultry may be served in this fashion, forming, when prettily garnished, a handsome luncheon or supper dish.

CHAPTER V.

TURKEYS.

Roast—boiled—braised—to serve cold—à la Provençale—à la Chipolata — galantine — marinaded —blanquette — hashed — minced — patties — devilled with sauce — pulled—rolled—croquettes—fried—soup—turkey poult—to re-dress.

Roast Turkey.—There are several different methods of preparing a turkey for roasting; some like it trussed in the same manner as a fowl, and roasted without stuffing. This will be ·found an excellent way for those who rather fear the richness of the forcemeat. The pure flavour of the bird is thus enjoyed without the addition of any other taste. When cooked in this way the turkey should be simply garnished with fresh watercress, and served with a little good brown gravy. The more popular method, however, of cooking a turkey is to stuff it either with veal forcemeat, chestnuts, or sausage-meat. Tie a buttered paper over the breast—after the bird is trussed, of course—and roast it before a clear hot fire, or in a well-heated brisk oven; the former is generally considered the best way, but it is not always convenient. Baste frequently while cooking, or the flesh will be dry and comparatively tasteless. Twenty minutes before the bird is done enough remove the paper from the breast, dredge a little flour over, and baste well to give a nice frothy appearance. Let it get well browned, and serve on a dish garnished with a ring of sausages, sliced lemon, and forcemeat balls. Brown gravy, and bread or chestnut sauce, should be sent to table as accompaniments. A small turkey requires an hour and a half to two hours to cook thoroughly.

Boiled Turkey.—Many persons consider this a pleasant change from roast turkey, especially about Christmas time, when the sight of the latter is apt to become monotonous. Choose a fine plump hen turkey, not too large, as the small or medium-sized ones are, generally speaking, more likely to be tender. Truss it as for boiling, and fill it with veal, oyster, chestnut, or onion stuffing; fasten the openings securely, and bind the bird round with tape to keep it firm. Put it in a buttered cloth sufficiently large to entirely cover it, then lay it in a saucepan and barely cover it with lukewarm water. Add a carrot cut in pieces, an onion stuck with four cloves, a few sticks of celery, a bunch of parsley, a teaspoonful of salt, and half a dozen peppercorns. Bring the water to a boil, then simmer gently until the turkey is tender, removing the scum occasionally as it rises to the surface. When done enough, take up the bird, and, after removing the cloth, place it on a hot dish; pour some good white sauce over, and garnish with sliced lemon and sprigs of parsley. Parsley and butter, plain melted butter, or oyster, chestnut, Dutch, or celery sauce, may be served with this dish. A boiled tongue, a small ham, or a piece of boiled bacon, are all suitable accompaniments to boiled turkey; they should be served on a separate dish, prettily garnished.

Braised Turkey.—This is an excellent method of

cooking an old turkey. Prepare the bird in the usual way, then cover it all over with. slices of fat bacon, securing them in their place with twine or narrow tape. Put a few slices of bacon at the bottom of a saucepan, lay the turkey on these, and add the giblets properly prepared, a calf's foot, some flavouring vegetables, and salt and pepper. Put more bacon over all, and nearly cover with stock. Put the lid on the pan, and let the contents simmer gently from four to six hours, according to the size and age of the bird. When sufficiently cooked remove the tape and bacon, and place the turkey on a hot dish ; pour over it a little white sauce, and garnish with tiny heaps of carrots and turnips cut into dice. It is best to boil some carrots and turnips separately for this purpose. More sauce should be sent to table in a tureen, or the liquor in which the turkey was boiled can be strained, slightly thickened, and served as gravy.

To serve Cold.—Pluck, singe, and draw a good-sized, plump turkey; bone it, and cut off the legs, but not the wings. Nearly fill it with nicely prepared veal forcemeat, or sausage meat, then push into the centre a small boiled tongue, which has been neatly trimmed about the root. Secure the openings of the bird firmly, and truss it, restoring it as nearly as possible to its original shape. Cook it according to the directions given for boiled turkey, taking care to simmer very gently lest the skin should burst. When done enough, set the bird in a cool place, and when quite cold mask it entirely over with good béchamel sauce. Place it on a dish and ornament it tastefully with sliced lemon, truffles, &c., garnish the edges of the dish with sprigs of fresh parsley, cut lemon, and clear aspic jelly. This forms a handsome dish for a cold supper. When a turkey is cooked in this fashion the carver must remember to cut the slices the cross way of the breast, thus giving to each person a slice composed of equal parts of turkey, tongue, and forcemeat.

Turkey à la Provençale.—Prepare a forcemeat as follows: Peel and parboil half a dozen large onions, drain and chop them, then put them into a saucepan with four ounces of butter, six ounces of breadcrumbs previously soaked in milk, a tablespoonful of finely chopped parsley, a teaspoonful of salt, half that quantity of pepper, the yolks of four fresh eggs, two tablespoonfuls of milk, and a few mushrooms chopped small. Stir this mixture over the fire until it becomes a rather firm paste, then use it to fill the turkey. Truss, and roast the bird in the usual way, and when done enough serve it with truffle or tomato sauce poured over, and send more sauce to table in a tureen.

Turkey à la Chipolata.—This is simply a turkey stuffed with sausage-meat or veal stuffing; it is then roasted in the ordinary way, and served with a chipolata ragoût, from which the dish takes its name. This ragoût is made in the following manner. Put into a stewpan the following ingredients, all previously cooked: small round sausages, half-inch squares of bacon or ham, button mushrooms, the red part of a carrot, and an equal quantity of turnip, scooped out in rounds no larger than peas, and some chestnuts, roasted, peeled, and cut in quarters. Use these in such proportions and quantities as are likely to be required. Pour over all some brown sauce, and if desired a glass of Madeira. Bring to a boil, then pour the ragoût round the turkey and serve.

E

Galantine of Turkey.—This dish is thought by some to be rather troublesome to prepare, but when nicely done it is so highly appreciated that one feels amply repaid for the labour entailed. Pluck, singe, and draw a nice turkey; divide it down the breast, cut off the wings and the neck, and bone it carefully without in any way injuring the skin. Remove part of the flesh from the inside of the bird and set it on one side. Lay the turkey flat on the table, skin downwards, and truss the legs inside; spread over it a layer of forcemeat about an inch thick, then put a layer of the meat cut from the turkey; upon this place some tiny slices of ham, boiled tongue, hard-boiled eggs, finely minced parsley, and a few truffles sliced. Season pleasantly with salt and pepper. The ingredients must be so arranged that the colours will contrast prettily, or when the galantine is cut the nice effect will be lost. Spread over all another layer of the sausage-meat; turn the skin over and roll the turkey in the form of a bolster, or thick sausage; sew it up very firmly to prevent the contents escaping, and cover the galantine with slices of fat bacon, cut thin. Tie it in a cloth and simmer gently for four or five hours in a saucepan with sufficient nicely-flavoured stock to cover it. The exact time must be regulated according to the size and age of the bird. Leave the galantine in the liquor till nearly cold, then place it between two dishes, put a heavy weight on the top and let it remain so until next day. Remove the cloth, free the galantine from any fat there may be about it, and brush it over with two or three coats of melted glaze, letting each coat dry before adding the next. Ornament tastefully with chopped aspic jelly, boiled beetroot cut out in fancy devices, hard-boiled eggs cut in quarters, and sprigs of fresh parsley.

Turkey Marinaded.—Parboil or half roast a young turkey, and when cold, divide it into neat joints; remove the bones, and restore the joints as nearly as possible to their original shape. Lay them to soak in a marinade made as follows: four table-spoonfuls of vinegar, the same quantity of water, two tablespoonfuls of salad oil, three small onions finely minced, a dessert-spoonful of salt, and a tea-spoonful of pepper. Mix these ingredients well and let the turkey lie for twelve hours, turning the joints now and again in order to season them equally all through. Drain them and dip each one in beaten egg, cover with powdered biscuits, and broil over a clear hot fire. Serve on a napkin, and garnish the dish with sliced lemon and fresh parsley. This dish is generally served dry, but some prefer it accompanied with mayonnaise sauce. (See Chap. VII.)

Blanquette of Turkey.—Cut the remains of a roast turkey into small neat slices; sprinkle over them a mixture of salt, pepper, grated lemon rind, and pounded mace, and set them on one side until wanted. Put the bones and trimming of the bird into a saucepan with two ounces of lean ham, an onion chopped fine, and sufficient stock or water to cover them. Let all simmer for an hour and a half, then strain the liquid into a clean saucepan; add a few tablespoonfuls of cream, half a teaspoonful of grated lemon rind, a little salt, and a pinch of cayenne. Let the sauce just reach boiling point, then lay in the slices of turkey and allow them to get thoroughly hot. After a few minutes stir in the yolks of two eggs well beaten, and continue stirring until the sauce begins to thicken nicely, but it must not on any account boil. Place a ring, or border, of well-mashed and seasoned potatoes round the edge of a hot dish, serve the blanquette in the centre, and garnish with toasted or fried sippets, and sprigs of fried parsley. This is a most dainty method of re-dressing the remains of any sort of poultry. It transforms mere scraps into quite a tempting little dish.

Hashed Turkey.—Cut the meat into neat pieces, dredge a little flour, nicely seasoned with pepper and salt, over them, and lay them in a saucepan; add about half a pint of stock, or good brown gravy, and allow the meat to become thoroughly hot. Add a spoonful of chopped mushrooms and a few drops of lemon juice. When simmered long enough, place the meat neatly on a hot dish, put some small forcemeat balls round about, and garnish with croutons and sprigs of parsley. Serve with the gravy poured over the meat.

Minced Turkey.—Free the meat entirely from skin, bones, and gristle, and mince it very finely. Put it into a saucepan with sufficient white sauce to thoroughly moisten it, and season pleasantly with salt, pepper, and pounded mace. If no white sauce is at hand, substitute a few tablespoonfuls of milk, an ounce of butter kneaded with an ounce of flour, and a teaspoonful of lemon juice. It is best to stir the lemon juice in just before serving. Let the mince simmer very gently by the side of the fire until quite hot, then turn it on to a dish, lay some carefully poached eggs on the top, and garnish with fried croutons. The mince must be just barely moistened or it will become sloppy.

Turkey Patties, or Vol-au-Vents.—Pick off any remains of white meat there may be left on the turkey, add to it a small proportion of ham, and mince both together very finely. Put the mince into a saucepan and barely moisten it with a little white stock. Stir gently over the fire for a minute or two, then add a tablespoonful of thick cream, and season rather highly with salt, cayenne, lemon rind, and pounded mace. When the mixture is thoroughly hot, use it to three-parts fill some small vol-au-vents, which have been made of good puff paste and baked separately. Arrange the vol-au-vents on a hot dish covered with a napkin, and garnished with fried parsley. If the vol-au-vents are considered too difficult to make, the mixture can be put into small patty tins, in which case the directions given for making chicken patties can be followed.

Devilled Turkey with Sauce.—Proceed in the same manner as directed for grilled chicken, and when sufficiently cooked, place the joints neatly on a hot dish and serve with a sauce made as follows: Cut three or four small onions into slices, and put them into a stewpan with as much strong vinegar as will moisten them. Let them simmer until quite soft, then add half a teacupful of good gravy, a pinch of cayenne, a pounded anchovy or a piece of anchovy butter, and if approved of, half a glass of wine. Stir in an ounce of fresh butter rolled in flour. Let the sauce boil gently for two or three minutes, then strain it carefully into the tureen or sauceboat. If preferred, the joints, after being prepared, may be gently stewed in the sauce instead of being grilled. When this plan is followed, the gravy is, of course, poured over the meat.

Pulled Turkey.—Take the legs and gizzard of a cold turkey, and prepare them in the same way as for

devilling. Remove the skin from the body of the
bird and pull off the remains of white meat with a
fork, in as long flakes as possible. Put the bones,
and all odd trimmings, into a saucepan with about
half a pint of stock, a finely minced onion, the rind
and juice of half a lemon, a little pounded mace, and
a sufficient seasoning of salt and pepper. Simmer
these slowly till the gravy is good and pleasantly
flavoured, then strain it into another saucepan; add
a little white roux, or butter rolled in flour, and a
small teacupful of milk or cream. Let this sauce
come to a boil, then lay in the white meat and allow
it to get quite hot. Dip the prepared legs and gizzard
in clarified butter, and broil them over a clear hot
fire. Put a wall of well-mashed potatoes on a dish
and brown it nicely, either in a hot oven, or before
the fire; pour the minced or pulled turkey in the
centre, arrange the legs and gizzard on the top, and
serve.

Rolled Turkey.—Divide a nice plump turkey
down the middle into two parts, remove the bones
without injuring the skin, and lay the pieces flat on
the table, skin downwards. Spread over each a layer
of nicely prepared forcemeat and roll them up tightly;
cover them with slices of rather fat bacon and secure
them with twine. Put the rolls into a saucepan, cover
them with good stock, and add a bunch of parsley, a
few sprigs of thyme, two small carrots cut in pieces,
a large onion stuck with half a dozen cloves, a blade
of mace, and a seasoning of salt and pepper. Let
the liquid reach boiling point, then simmer gently
until the turkey is sufficiently cooked. This is a most
convenient dish, as it may be served either hot or
cold ; and either way it is equally delicious. If it is
to be eaten hot, place the rolls on a dish, and remove

the twine ; strain, and, if necessary, thicken the sauce. Pour part of it over the meat and send the rest to table in a tureen.   If, however, the dish is to be served cold, allow the rolls to lie in the liquor for an hour, then afterwards, when quite cold, remove the twine, and brush them over with a few coats of glaze. Garnish'with sliced lemon, aspic jelly roughly chopped, and sprigs of fresh parsley.

Turkey Croquettes.—Take the remains of either roast or boiled turkey, free the meat from skin, &c., and mince it finely. Supposing there are six ounces, mix with it two ounces of lean ham, or tongue, and half a dozen button mushrooms, also minced. Put an ounce of butter into a stewpan, and as it melts stir in gradually an ounce of flour. When quite smooth add a few tablespoonfuls of stock, and two or three of cream; continue stirring until the flour is thoroughly cooked, then draw the pan on one side and add the mince, with a teaspoonful of strained lemon juice, salt, pepper, and a little mace. Mix all these ingredients well, then turn the preparation out on a plate to cool. When quite cold make it up into any shape which may be desired—cutlets, corks, balls, diamonds, or any other pretty device which may suggest itself. Brush these over with beaten egg, cover with fine bread crumbs, and fry in plenty of boiling fat till lightly browned. Serve arranged in a circle, and fill in the centre with fresh crisp watercress or fried parsley. In order to cook these and similar little dainties satisfactorily, a frying-basket should be used. They can be done in a fryingpan, but the process is rather a difficult one, but with a basket it is quite easy.

Fried Turkey.—Divide the remains of a cold

roast turkey into neat joints, or pieces; dip these in
beaten egg, cover with crumbs or crushed biscuits,
and fry in boiling fat until nicely browned and crisp.
Arrange the pieces neatly on a bed of any well cooked,
suitable vegetables, and pour round about—but not
over—a very dainty sauce made as follows: Put the
bones and trimmings of the bird into a saucepan with
stock, or water to cover them; add a bunch of parsley,
a few sticks of celery, a carrot cut in pieces, an onion,
half a dozen cloves, half a dozen peppercorns, and
salt. Simmer these for an hour or more, then strain
the liquor and carefully free it from all fat. Put an
ounce of butter into a stewpan and fry in it two
ounces of lean minced ham; dredge a little flour over
the ham, and stir briskly for a few minutes until well
browned, but not at all burnt. Add the strained
gravy from the bones, &c.; let it just reach boiling
point, then it is ready for use.

Turkey Soup, Economical.—After all the meat
of the turkey has been used for patties, croquettes,
rissoles, mince, &c., gather the bones together, break
them in small pieces, and put them into a saucepan
with any forcemeat there may be left, and pour over
them about two quarts of stock; add some salt, a
few sticks of celery, two carrots cut in pieces, a large
onion, a bunch of herbs, a dozen peppercorns, and
three or four cloves. Bring the liquid to a boil, skim
carefully, and simmer gently until the bones are perfectly clean. Strain the soup into another saucepan,
free it from all fat, and add more seasoning if required. The soup may be thickened—if thick soup
is preferred—with a little arrowroot, ground rice, or
a handful of bread crumbs. Drop a little vermicelli,
macaroni, or tinned vegetables into it; boil it up for a
minute, then serve. Toasted bread, cut into dice,

may be served as an accompaniment. If a rich soup is desired, it can be made according to the directions given for chicken soup, using one turkey instead of two chickens. The remains of a cold turkey may also be potted, scalloped, made into fritters, rissoles, and sandwiches, by following the recipes given for chicken.

Turkey Poult.—This is an excellent substitute for a full-grown bird. It is most easily obtained during summer and autumn, when the large turkeys are out of season, which renders it very acceptable. It is customary to roast them in the same manner as a fully-grown bird, but they are not generally stuffed. Truss them with the head tucked under the wing, and the legs twisted under, like a duck; the feet should be left on, but the claws must be cut off. Put an ounce of butter mixed with a dessert-spoonful of minced parsley into the inside of the bird, secure the openings, and baste liberally whilst cooking. Garnish the dish with watercress, and serve with bread sauce and good brown gravy.

The Same, to Re-dress.—The remains of a turkey poult may be dressed according to any of the recipes given for a large turkey, or a more delicate method still is the following: Cut the meat as neatly as possible, and free it from bones, skin, and sinew; put the bones and trimmings into a saucepan with a pint of white stock, a few sprigs of parsley, an onion minced very finely, six mushrooms chopped small, a blade of mace, and a few cloves. Add salt and pepper to taste, and simmer the sauce until pleasantly flavoured. Strain it into another saucepan, thicken slightly with white roux, and add a few spoonfuls of good cream. Stir over the fire till the sauce boils, then add the pieces of turkey, and let them barely simmer till hot through. Serve the meat on a hot dish with the sauce poured over. Garnish with croutons, sliced lemon, and sprigs of parsley.

CHAPTER VI.

FOWLS IN GENERAL.

À la Hollandaise — à la Mayonnaise — à l'Indienne — à la Milanaise — quenelles à la béchamel — fillets in batter — Guinea-fowls — ornamental poultry.

Fowls à la Hollandaise.—Prepare a large plump fowl in the usual way, then remove the breast-bone and fill up the cavity thus made with a dainty forcemeat prepared as follows: Boil a medium-sized onion until nearly soft, then chop it very small, and mix with it a breakfast-cupful of finely sifted crumbs, two ounces of beef suet chopped small, a dessert-spoonful of minced parsley, half a teaspoonful of lemon-juice, and a sufficient seasoning of salt and pepper. Mix these ingredients thoroughly, and bind them together with beaten egg, cover the breast of the fowl with buttered paper, and roast in a brisk oven, or before a clear hot fire. When half cooked remove the paper, and pour over the bird some good frying batter; let this get dry, then pour some more over, continuing in this way until the fowl is thickly and evenly coated. It should, when finished, be nicely browned and crisp. Serve on a hot dish, garnished with cut lemon, and sprigs of parsley, and accompanied with Hollandaise sauce.

Fowl à la Mayonnaise.—Cut up a cold roast or

boiled fowl into joints a convenient size for serving.
Place a layer of carefully washed lettuce, cut small, on
a dish ; arrange on this the inferior parts of the fowl,
and cover with a layer of hard-boiled eggs, ancho-
vies, cucumber, and boiled beetroot, all chopped into
dice and mixed. Put next another layer of salad,
chopped radishes, spring onions, small cress, endive,
&c., and last of all arrange the remainder of the
fowl, taking care to allow all the different colours to
appear. Garnish the dish with hard-boiled eggs cut
in rings, slices, or quarters, and fancy shapes of
beetroot. Just before serving mask the whole with
Mayonnaise sauce, and sprinkle over the top a little
lobster coral which has been pounded and sifted.
If prepared with good taste this is a most attractive
dish.

Fowl à l'Indienne.—Put a dessert-spoonful of
curry powder, the same quantity of curry paste, and
a teaspoonful of ground rice or cornflour into a
basin, mix to a smooth paste with a little cold water,
and stir in gradually a pint of boiling stock. Pour
this into a saucepan, and stir it over the fire until it
becomes rather thick and quite smooth. Have ready
a nice tender fowl prepared in the usual way, and
cut up into neat joints a convenient size for serving;
fry these in hot butter until nicely browned, then lay
them into the curry sauce ; add a whole onion stuck
with half a dozen cloves, cover the pan closely, and
allow the contents to simmer slowly till the fowl is
sufficiently cooked. Put a border of carefully prepared rice round the edge of a hot dish, upon which
place some baked tomatoes ; arrange the fowl in the
centre, remove the onion, pour the sauce over, and
serve very hot. If preferred, the tomatoes may be
rubbed through a sieve and added to the sauce. A

teaspoonful of lemon-juice, added just at the last moment, is considered by some to be a great improvement.

Fowl à la Milanaise.—Mix together on a plate, or a sheet of white paper, two ounces of grated Parmesan cheese, four tablespoonfuls of sifted breadcrumbs, half a teaspoonful of salt, and a pinch of cayenne. Cut up a fowl into neat fillets, and dip each one first into well-beaten egg, then into the seasoned crumbs, press the mixture firmly into the meat, and fry the fillets in hot butter until sufficiently cooked and delicately browned. Serve on a bed of well-cooked vegetables, surrounded with a Milanese ragoût. The ragoût is made as follows : Take any odd pieces of fowl and cut them into dice about half an inch square, mix with them an equal quantity of tongue, ham, and macaroni, a few mushrooms, and truffles, if obtainable, all cut small ; also the red part of a carrot cut into tiny balls about the size of a pea. Put these ingredients, in such quantities as are likely to be required, into a saucepan with a little good white sauce, a tablespoonful of grated cheese (Parmesan), a seasoning of pepper, and a little grated nutmeg. Toss the ragoût lightly over the fire for a few minutes until thoroughly hot, when it is ready for use.

Quenelles à la béchamel.—Carefully pick off all the remains of meat from one or two roast fowls ; free it from every particle of skin and gristle, and pass it through a sausage machine. If a machine is not at hand, the meat must be minced as finely as possible, pounded in a mortar, and then, with a wooden spoon, it must be patiently pressed through a wire sieve. Supposing there are three-quarters of a

pound of meat, mix with it four ounces of breadcrumbs soaked in milk and drained, four tablespoonfuls of good white sauce, a sufficient seasoning of
salt, cayenne, and mace, and two well-beaten eggs.
Put the mixture into a saucepan, and beat it over
the fire until the ingredients are thoroughly mixed
and quite hot. Spread the preparation on a plate,
and when cold form it into small oval balls. Poach
these in hot fat in the usual way, or, if preferred,
the quenelles may be egged, breadcrumbed, and
fried. In either case, serve them firmly planted on
a bed of mashed potatoes, and over the whole pour
some good béchamel sauce. If the quenelles are to
be poached, it is a good plan to test a small portion
of the mixture before proceeding with the rest. If
the forcemeat prove too solid, a little water or stock
may be added; if not firm enough, the addition of
another egg will probably render it of the right
consistency. The great secret of making these
dainty little tit-bits successfully, lies in having the
ingredients thoroughly pounded. The preparation
should be perfectly smooth before we attempt to
cook it.

Fillets of Fowl in Batter.—Cut as many neat
fillets as possible out of the remains of a cold roast
fowl; they may be cut any size or shape, but they
look prettiest when small. Put them together in
pairs with a layer of finely minced cooked ham between, and press them firmly to make them adhere.
Sprinkle them entirely over with a mixture of salt,
pepper, pounded mace, and grated lemon rind.
Press this gently into the fillets, dip each into some
rich frying batter, and fry in plenty of boiling fat.
When done they should be a golden brown and
quite crisp; drain them carefully from all fat, and

serve them neatly arranged on a folded napkin. Garnish the dish with fried parsley.

Guinea Fowls.—The flavour of a Guinea fowl improves considerably by being kept, therefore let the bird hang as long as possible before being cooked. It may be trussed like a turkey, but the head may be left on if desired. Lard the breast closely with strips of fat bacon—the proper larding bacon—and put a small lump of butter mixed with chopped parsley inside. The flesh of a Guinea fowl is rather dry, therefore the bird must be almost constantly basted while cooking. It is best when roasted before the fire, as then the basting is a very simple matter; but if this cannot be managed, it may, with care, be done very nicely in a brisk oven. Serve with rich brown gravy and bread sauce. The dish may be garnished with fresh watercress, the same as for turkey poult.

Ornamental Poultry.—Small turkeys, pheasants, partridges, and chickens, are all suitable for cooking in the following manner. Boil the birds, and when cold, mask them entirely over with good béchamel sauce made very thick. Place the birds on a dish, and ornament their breasts with prettily cut designs of tongue, lean ham, beetroot, or black truffles. Garnish round the edge of the dish with chopped aspic jelly and sprigs of fresh parsley. If more convenient, the birds may be cut into small neat joints previous to being masked with the sauce; but they form a most attractive dish when kept whole.

CHAPTER VII.

SAUCES AND GRAVIES.

Apple—béchamel—bread—celery—chestnut—Dutch—egg—gooseberry—mushroom—Mayonnaise—onion—oyster—parsley—sorrel—tomato—white sauce—gravies—Hollandaise—glaze.

IT is not enough that we know how to select, truss, and cook our fowls. There is still something else to be learnt, that is, how to prepare the sauce, or gravy suitable to serve as an accompaniment. The most costly, carefully cooked dish may be improved by the addition of a really well-made sauce, while by the same means, the most ordinary, everyday fare may be rendered quite dainty. Soyer used to say that "Sauces are to cookery what grammar is to language, and the gamut to music;" and we think he was right. They are really indispensable if we mean our cookery to be a success. If, however, sauces are not nicely made, it is better to dispense with them altogether, for in that case they simply spoil the dish which they accompany. For instance, nothing can well be more disagreeable than to have sauce, or gravy, sent to table half cold, ornamented on the top with a cake of fat; or a sauce which is intended to be smooth, served with lumps in it. It always seems to me a great pity to have things which are so simple, and easy to make, completely spoiled just for lack of proper care and attention.

One of the best methods of extracting the fat from sauce, or gravy, is the following : when the sauce has boiled up, strain it through a piece of coarse muslin previously soaked in cold water ; the coldness of the cloth will instantly congeal the fat, allowing only the pure gravy to pass through. After any thickening, or flavouring, has been added, the sauce must be allowed to boil up for a minute or two, in order to blend everything nicely together. It is easy to remember that all hot sauces should be served *quite* hot, and that in every case the flavour of the sauce ought to contrast pleasantly with the dish which it is to accompany. The following are some of the most popular sauces and gravies used as accompaniments to poultry.

Apple Sauce.—Peel, core, and slice half a dozen good cooking apples, place them in a saucepan over a gentle fire, and add just enough water to keep them from burning. Let them simmer slowly, stirring frequently, until the fruit is reduced to a pulp ; then turn them into a bowl and beat them well with a wooden spoon until perfectly smooth. Add two heaped tablespoonfuls of sugar, an ounce of butter, and a few drops of lemon juice. Mix well and serve hot.

Béchamel Sauce.—Put a quart of white stock into a saucepan with an onion, cut in pieces, a few mushrooms, or a little mushroom powder, a bunch of savoury herbs, and a small teaspoonful of salt. Let these boil together till the flavour of the herbs has been fully extracted and the stock is reduced to about half the quantity, then strain it into another saucepan, an enamelled one if possible. Add a gill of good cream mixed smoothly with a tablespoonful

F

of arrowroot; simmer gently over a slow fire, stirring all the time, until the sauce thickens, when it is ready for use. When this sauce is wanted for coating cold fowls of any description, it must be made sufficiently thick to adhere to the birds, therefore a little less stock should be used in making the sauce, and a little more arrowroot and cream.

Bread Sauce.—Put two ounces of stale breadcrumbs into a saucepan with half a pint of milk; drop into the centre a whole onion, peeled and stuck with half a dozen peppercorns, and let the sauce boil very gently for ten minutes, stirring constantly to prevent burning. When taken from the fire, remove the onion and the peppercorns, stir in an ounce of fresh butter, a little salt, and two or three spoonfuls of cream; keep on stirring until the butter is entirely dissolved, then serve the sauce in a tureen.

Celery Sauce.—Cut the white part of two heads of celery, and divide them into pieces an inch long. Put three ounces of butter in a stewpan, and when it is melted throw in the celery, with an onion sliced thin, and stew very gently till tender. Mix in very smoothly a teaspoonful of flour, and when it has browned a little, add a breakfast-cupful of good gravy, some salt, pepper, and a grating of nutmeg. Rub the whole through a sieve, make hot, and serve.

Chestnut Sauce.—Roast a dozen chestnuts until tender, then remove the brown rind and the thin skin underneath, and put the nuts into a mortar with a teaspoonful of salt, half that quantity of pepper, a teaspoonful of sifted sugar, a teaspoonful of lemon juice, and an ounce of butter. Pound these ingredients to a smooth paste, and mix it with a breakfast-cupful of milk, or cream if obtainable; put the mixture into a saucepan, and stir it over the fire until the liquid boils. This is white chestnut sauce; if brown sauce is preferred, use good brown gravy instead of milk or cream. The white sauce is generally served with boiled fowls, the brown with roast fowls.

Dutch Sauce.—Put four ounces of butter, the yolks of three eggs well beaten, a teaspoonful of ground rice, and a dessert-spoonful of lemon juice into an earthenware jar or a pipkin; set this into a saucepan containing boiling water, and stir constantly until the butter melts. Continue stirring for ten or fifteen minutes, till the sauce becomes thick and creamy, but it must not be allowed to boil or it will curdle, and so be completely spoiled. If a rather sour, sharp flavour is liked, a spoonful of vinegar may be added just before serving. Generally used to accompany boiled fowls.

Egg Sauce.—Put half a pint of white stock into a saucepan; add two ounces of butter into which has been kneaded two dessert-spoonfuls of flour. Stir the sauce till it boils, then add some finely minced parsley, three hard-boiled eggs chopped into dice, a little salt, a pinch of cayenne, and a teaspoonful of lemon juice. If a very rich sauce is required, another ounce of butter may be stirred in after the pan is removed from the fire. Sometimes the whites only of the eggs are used for the sauce; then the yolks are rubbed through a sieve and sprinkled over the breast of the fowl.

Gooseberry Sauce.—Cut the tops and tails from half a pint of green gooseberries; boil them gently

until tender, then press them through a sieve, and
stir them into half a pint of good plain melted butter.
Season to taste with ginger and grated lemon rind,
and add also a little fine sugar if required.

Hollandaise Sauce.—Put three ounces of butter
into a saucepan, and as it melts, stir in an ounce of
flour; beat the mixture, with the back of a small
wooden spoon, until perfectly smooth, then add half
a pint of milk.   Stir constantly until the sauce boils,
then draw the pan on one side, and add the yolks of
two eggs, well beaten, and two tablespoonfuls of
some thoroughly cooked vegetables, such as carrots,
turnips, cucumber, &c.   The vegetables must be
stamped out in very small, pretty shapes.   Add a
seasoning of salt and pepper to taste, and stir the
sauce by the side of the fire for a few minutes longer,
but great care must be taken to see that it does not
boil.   If this point is neglected, the eggs will speedily
form into lumps, thus rendering the sauce unfit for
use.

Mayonnaise Sauce.—To make this sauce both
time and patience are required.   Put the yolk of one
fresh egg into a basin, and beat it with a fork until it
becomes thick; add a saltspoonful each of salt, pepper, and dry mustard, and when these ingredients are
thoroughly mixed, half a pint of fine salad oil and a
quarter of a pint of the best vinegar must be added.
The oil must be added in drops at first, afterwards in
teaspoonfuls, the beating to be kept up all the time,
and after every two spoonfuls of oil, a teaspoonful
of vinegar must be added.   Just at the last, a tablespoonful of lemon juice may be stirred in to give it a
nice sharp flavour.   If this sauce is made too quickly
it is sure to curdle, and will not be at all nice.

Mushroom Sauce.—Thoroughly cleanse the mushrooms from any soil or grit that hangs about them ; rub the tops over with a piece of flannel dipped in salt in order to remove the skin, then cut off the stalks. Chop the mushrooms very small and simmer them for twenty minutes in good brown stock, or gravy. Add an ounce of butter rolled in flour, and flavour with lemon juice if approved of. Stir the sauce until the butter is entirely dissolved, then serve. If white mushroom sauce is preferred, prepare the mushrooms in precisely the same manner, but simmer them in béchamel sauce instead of brown stock.

Onion Sauce.—Peel, and cut into quarters, two large Spanish onions, or what would be equal to them in ordinary onions ; put them into a saucepan with plenty of cold water and boil them until tender. Drain off all the water, and chop the onions very finely ; put them into a clean saucepan with a pint of milk with which has been smoothly mixed two ounces of butter and an ounce and a half of flour, and add salt and pepper to taste. Stir the sauce over the fire for ten minutes, and serve very hot.

Oyster Sauce.—If made from fresh oysters, open about a dozen, being careful not to waste a drop of the liquor. Put this latter into a scrupulously clean saucepan with half a pint of milk, an ounce of butter rolled in flour, a small piece of lemon rind, a seasoning of pounded mace, and a tiny pinch of cayenne. Stir till the sauce comes to a boil, then draw the pan on one side and add a few spoonfuls of cream, or if this is not convenient, two egg yolks, well beaten, may be used instead. Continue stirring until the sauce becomes thick and smooth, then just two or three minutes previous to serving, remove the lemon

rind and stir in the oysters, which have been bearded
and chopped small. Great care must be taken to see
that the sauce does not boil after the eggs or oysters
are added, or it will be completely spoiled.

Parsley   Sauce.—Take a handful of fresh
parsley, wash it thoroughly and pick off the leaves.
Boil these quickly in salt and water for two minutes,
then chop them as finely as possible. Stir them into
half a pint of well-made melted butter, or white sauce,
and serve in a tureen.

Sorrel Sauce.—Pick the stalks and large fibres
from a quart of fresh green sorrel ; wash it in several
waters until thoroughly clean, then put it into a very
clean saucepan with two ounces of butter and stew it
slowly till quite tender, stirring frequently to prevent
it burning. When done enough, rub it through a
coarse sieve ; season with salt and pepper, and add
sufficient cream to make the sauce of the right consistency. Serve very hot.

Tomato Sauce.—Take as many ripe tomatoes
as are likely to be required ; cut them in halves,
squeeze out the seeds and the juice, and put the
tomatoes into a saucepan with a tablespoonful of
finely minced lean ham, cooked previously ; a few
sprigs of parsley, thyme, and a bay-leaf tied together ;
a sufficient seasoning of salt and pepper, a small
onion, or two shallots, sliced very thin, and enough
good gravy to moisten the whole. Stir these ingredients over the fire till the tomatoes are quite soft,
then remove the herbs, and gently press everything
else through a sieve. Return the pulp to the saucepan, and stir again until the sauce is quite hot. It

may then be served either in a tureen or poured round about the fowl.

White Sauce.—Put into a small saucepan two ounces of butter, and as it melts, mix in very smoothly two ounces of flour, using the back of a small wooden spoon to stir with. When the flour is sufficiently cooked, add gradually a pint of milk, salt, pepper, and grated nutmeg or pounded mace. Stir the sauce constantly until it boils, then strain it carefully, and it is ready. If a richer sauce is required it can easily be obtained by using part cream, or the yolks of eggs well beaten.

Gravies.—For ordinary everyday use, a good cook or an experienced housewife will seldom, if ever, require gravy beef from which to make gravy. The giblets, bones, and trimmings of meat and poultry, thoroughly cleaned and well stewed, will generally suffice for the purpose. Let them be stewed while quite fresh, and the stock thus obtained strained into an earthenware vessel until wanted. Flavouring vegetables should be boiled in the stock to make it really good: carrots, turnips, celery, onions, with a bunch of savoury herbs, are the most suitable for this purpose. They should be cut into pieces, and if brown stock is required they must be fried in hot fat until brightly coloured, previous to their being added to the stock. When very superior white stock is needed, it is best made from the bones of poultry, veal bones, and a cow heel, or calf's foot.

When the stock is once obtained it is easily transformed into gravy by the addition of certain flavouring and thickening ingredients, and these, of course, should always be in perfect harmony with the dish which they are to accompany. For instance, the rich

brown gravy generally served with roast chickens, or
turkeys, is simply good brown stock thickened with
brown thickening, and flavoured with whatever seasoning the housewife may prefer; while the white
sauces, or gravies, are simply white stock thickened
with white thickening, and flavoured according to
taste. The thickening in both cases is composed
of the same ingredients, namely, flour and butter,
and the mode of mixing is the same. They are put
into a small stewpan and beaten with a wooden spoon
over the fire until they form a thick smooth paste,
only in one case the preparation is allowed to become
a dark brown colour, while in the other it is kept
perfectly white. The flour and butter are generally
used in equal quantities. Some housewives keep
a supply of these commodities on hand, which is
a most commendable plan, but where this is not the
case the butter kneaded with flour may be used as
directed.

It must always be remembered that sauces, such
as Worcester, &c., and all ingredients used for
flavouring, should be added to the gravy only a short
time before serving, as their strength speedily
evaporates, and they should also be used very carefully. It is always wise to add too little rather than
too much, as it is an easy matter to add more if
required, whereas if too much is put in at first, it is
totally impossible to take it out. A delicious gravy
for ducks or géese can be made as follows: slice a
large onion very thin, and fry it, until well browned,
in about an ounce of butter, or good beef dripping. Add a breakfast-cupful of brown stock, half
a teaspoonful of powdered sage, salt, and pepper if necessary, and a pinch of cayenne. Simmer
slowly for half an hour, then strain the gravy into
another saucepan, thicken it if a thick gravy is

preferred, stir in a glass of port or claret, and serve very hot.

Liquid browning is a very useful thing to keep on hand for colouring gravies when they are not wanted thick. It is soon made, and if stored in a cool dry place will keep good for a long time. Put two ounces of common brown sugar into a saucepan with a table-spoonful of water, and set it on the fire to boil. As soon as the sugar begins to acquire colour, lessen the heat by drawing the pan on one side, and continue stir-ring with a wooden spoon, until by degrees it becomes nearly black, without being in the least burnt. When sufficiently baked, pour on a pint of warm water, boil for a few minutes, then carefully skim it, and when quite cold bottle it for future use. A few drops of this added to a pale, rather poor-looking gravy, will be found a decided improvement. It greatly enriches the appearance of the gravy, without in any way interfering with the flavour.

Glaze.—This is made from clear stock boiled down until it forms a strong jelly; the knuckle of veal, the legs and shins of beef, and shanks of mutton are the most suitable to use for this purpose, being par-ticularly gelatinous. As a rule, I always prefer home-made articles to those which we purchase ready for use, but glaze certainly forms an exception to this rule. On an average, a pound of meat is required to make an ounce of glaze, therefore it will be seen at a glance that it is rather an expensive item. It can, however, be bought at any good grocers for less than half the cost of making it at home. It is usually sold in skins, and will, if kept in a cool dry place, keep good for a considerable time. A small portion can be cut off and melted down as required. To melt the glaze, put it in a jar, and place the latter in

a larger vessel containing boiling water, taking care
that the water does not reach to the top of the jar.
The surface of the meat must always be perfectly
dry previous to the glaze being put on; and one
coating must be allowed to stiffen before another is
added. Three coatings are generally required to
impart a clear, bright appearance.

CHAPTER VIII.

HINTS ON TRUSSING AND CARVING.

WHEN a fowl has been well and properly trussed, it is a great help to the carver, rendering the operation quite easy and pleasant to perform; but if the first part of the business has been done awkwardly, the carving becomes a much more difficult matter. To truss a bird nicely for boiling, proceed as follows: Pluck, draw, singe, and wipe it well inside and out with a clean damp cloth. Cut off the neck even with the back, but leave sufficient length of skin to fold neatly over. Remove the feet and draw the legs inside. This is considered by some cooks rather a difficult thing to accomplish; but, with a little practice, it soon becomes quite easy. Insert two fingers into the body of the bird, and gradually loosen the flesh from the leg-bones by working the fingers gently round. When this is done, it is a very simple matter to press in the bones. Secure the wings firmly to the sides by means of a small skewer, and pass a string over the top to keep it in its place. Fold the skin of the neck neatly, and fasten it also with a skewer. Make a tiny slit in the apron, through which the rump must be put, then the fowl is ready.

When the bird is going to be roasted, the method

of trussing is rather different. Pluck, draw, singe, and wipe it, same as for boiling, but be careful to use only white paper when singeing it. Scald and scrape the legs, cut off the claws, and fasten both pinions and legs firmly to the body of the bird; in doing this use skewers long enough to go right through the fowl, and secure them well with string. Put the liver, nicely cleaned, in one wing, the gizzard, skinned and emptied, in the other. To make the bird feel firm, and look a good shape, pass a trussing-needle, threaded with string, through the middle of the body, and fasten it securely on either side. The skewers, of course, must always be taken out before the fowl is sent to table.

Ducks are generally trussed like fowls, but sometimes it is preferred to leave the feet on, in which case they must first be scalded, then skinned, and twisted round till they lie flat on the back of the bird.

Geese and turkeys for boiling, are trussed according to the directions given for boiled fowls; but for roasting, the breast-bone must be broken by beating it with a rolling-pin. This gives a much more plump appearance to the bird. Sometimes the backbone, too, is broken in order to make the bird lie flat, and steady on the dish. The legs and wings of a goose are trussed in the same manner as those of a fowl, but the feet of a turkey are generally left on. They are twisted round on to the back of the bird, after being properly cleaned by scalding and scraping. The nose must be very securely fastened through the slit made in the apron, or the stuffing will be very apt to escape during the process of cooking.

And now just a few words about the business of carving. There is no reason in the world why we should think that this art—for an art it certainly is—belongs exclusively to gentlemen; yet we seem, somehow or other, to have got that idea. A housewife, in the absence of her lord and master, may often be called upon to perform this duty herself; then how exceedingly awkward she feels if she has not previously accustomed herself to it. It is always wise, I think, for us to know how a thing should be done, whether or not we are called upon to do it. At any rate, it renders us competent to act in a case of emergency, should one happen to arise. After all, if we attack the business with full confidence in our own powers, it is a very simple affair—that is, as I said before, if the birds have been properly trussed.

If we are to do our work with credit and comfort to ourselves, we must, of necessity, have the right tools to work with; therefore, in the carving of poultry a game, or poultry carver, is indispensable. These knives, which are short and thick, and pointed and sharp at the end, do the work neatly and clean, and are an immense help to the carver. Chickens, fowls, and ducks are carved in precisely the same way. Insert the knife between the leg and the body, and cut right through to the bone; then turn the leg back, and if the bird is young the joint will give way at once. The wings are taken off in the same manner; then, the four quarters having been removed, cut off the merrythought and the neck-bones. These last are removed by pressing the knife in near the neck, when they will break off quite easily. Next separate the breast from the body of the fowl by cutting through the tender ribs close to the breast, quite down to the tail. Now turn the bird back upwards, and put the knife into the bone midway between the neck and the rump, when on raising the lower end it will separate quite easily. Turn

the rump from you, and take off very neatly the two
sidesmen, which completes the operation. The breast
and wings of a fowl are considered the best parts,
but in very young birds the legs are the most juicy.
A boiled fowl is carved much in the same way as a
roast fowl.

Geese and turkeys are carved rather differently.
The breast is so large that slices taken from it, and
from the wings, generally suffice for the company.
They should be cut from each side alternately,
beginning close to the wings. A little of the forcemeat, or stuffing, should be served to each guest,
and if it is necessary for the legs to be served, they
should be removed as directed for fowls, and be cut
in slices. But it must be remembered that they,
with the gizzard, will make an excellent devil if they
can, by any means, be preserved.

INDEX.

PRINTED BY J. S. VIRTUE AND CO., LIMITED, CITY ROAD, LONDON.

G

HOUSEHOLD MANUALS.

Price 2s.

SHOWELL'S

HOUSEKEEPER'S ACCOUNT BOOK

FOR THE YEAR 1888.

WITH ENTIRELY NEW

INTRODUCTORY HINTS

ON

HOUSEHOLD ECONOMY.

By Miss M. L. ALLEN,

AUTHOR OF "BREAKFAST DISHES," "SAVOURIES AND SWEETS."

"A useful household diary."—*Graphic.*

"The arrangement is so complete that few establishments will fail to find it adequate."—*The Queen.*

"One of the most complete works of the kind issued."
Daily Chronicle.

"It is also a day-book and cash-book, excellently planned."
Glasgow Herald.

"Some excellent practical hints on household economy."
Christian World.

"For the housewife who wants to be thrifty and methodical, but does not know how, it must be a still greater boon."
Scotsman.

N.B.—The Volume for 1889 will be published in December, 1888, and will contain a complete revision of the Quarterly Expenditure Tables.

LONDON: J. S. VIRTUE & Co., Limited, 26, IVY LANE.

USEFUL 1s. HOUSEHOLD MANUALS.

15,000th. 1s.; Limp cloth, 1s. 6d.

BREAKFAST DISHES

For Every Morning of Three Months.

By Miss M. L. ALLEN.

"The question 'What shall we have for breakfast?' is here answered in a practical way."—*The Queen.*

"A housewife armed with this little manual need never be at a loss to know what to order for the first meal of the day."—*The Literary World.*

"The writer gives an appetising breakfast bill of fare for every morning extending over a period of three months. To housekeepers this little book is invaluable."—*Paper and Printing Trades Journal.*

"The book is a suggestive and useful one, and will no doubt prove acceptable to cooks and housewives anxious to break away from the existing stereotyped routine of the breakfast fare."—*Newcastle Weekly Chronicle.*

"We have no hesitation in heartily commending this little book."—*Yorkshire Post.*

"A useful manual for young housekeepers and others."—*Bookseller.*

"Supplies a long-felt want by housekeepers."—*Graphic.*

"The housekeeper must be hard to please who does not find something to suit both her taste and her purse."—*Dundee Advertiser.*

LONDON: J. S. VIRTUE & CO., Limited, 26, IVY LANE.

Orders received at all Booksellers.

TWELFTH THOUSAND.

SAVOURIES AND SWEETS.

By Miss M. L. ALLEN.

Price 1s. ; or limp cloth, silver gilt, 1s. 6d.

"Of great merit."—*Saturday Review.*

"Miss Allen's receipts are distinct as well as varied."
Liverpool Courier.

"More useful than many of its more pretentious rivals."
The Lady.

"So very adequate is this manual in its way, that its cost will be begrudged by but comparatively few householders."
Western Daily Mercury.

"The mysteries of omelettes, tarts, fritters, &c., are here made clear to the understanding of any novice in cookery."
The Tablet.

Cloth boards, silver gilt, 2s. 6d.

SAVOURY DISHES,

BEING

BREAKFAST DISHES & SAVOURIES AND SWEETS

BOUND UP IN ONE VOLUME.

LONDON: J. S. VIRTUE & CO., Limited, 26, IVY LANE.

USEFUL *1s.* HOUSEHOLD MANUALS.

FIFTH THOUSAND.

ECONOMICAL

FRENCH COOKERY for LADIES.

By A CORDON-BLEU.

Price 1s.; or limp cloth, silver gilt, 1s. 6d.

"Very useful and also readable. . . . We like her little book."—*Athenæum.*

"For a cookery book the work is singularly lively and unconventional."—*Yorkshire Post.*

"'First-rate Receipts.'—Such an announcement is always satisfactory to the receiver. Everybody can participate in such receipts by laying out one shilling on a little book by Cordon Bleu, called 'Economical French Cookery for Ladies.' There's no speculation about it. It's a certainty. The authoress *ne fait pas une bonne farce* with her readers, though she does with some of her dishes. 'Plates' and 'Cuts' will be supplied by the readers. The book is treated with as light a touch as a cook shou'd employ in making good pastry, and will be substantially useful to the Household Brigade generally."—*Punch.*

"Her instructions are clear and concise."
Galignani's Messenger.

"The lectures are very interesting, containing many receipts for delicious soups and dishes."—*Liverpool Courier.*

"We are agreeably surprised to find that the author has departed from the conventional cut and dried style of cookery books. . . . All ladies will be grateful for the splendid list of menus."—*Western Daily Mercury.*

"Those who are enamoured of French cookery—and who is not?—cannot wish for a better introduction to its mysteries than that offered by this pleasantly written book."—*Literary World.*

"A handy little volume."—*Glasgow Herald.*

LONDON: J. S. VIRTUE & CO., Limited, 26, IVY LANE.

New and Attractive Children's Books,

PROFUSELY ILLUSTRATED.

Price 1s. each.

Bound in Pictorial Boards, varnished.

PAUL LUGGERSHALL.

BY W. H. KINGSTON.

A TALE OF ADVENTURE FOR BOYS.

OUR NOAH'S ARK.

A COLLECTION OF SHORT STORIES SUITABLE FOR YOUNG
CHILDREN.

STORIES OF FOREIGN LANDS.

FOR LITTLE FOLK AT HOME.

SHORT STORIES FOR SUNDAY READING.

A COLLECTION OF INTERESTING TALES SUITABLE
FOR SUNDAY.

Price 5s. each.

Handsomely bound in cloth gilt, gilt edges.
About 256 pages and 200 Illustrations in each Vol.

MY PLEASURE BOOK.

BY THE WINTER'S FIRE. [*In the press.*

PLEASANT STORIES.

CHILDREN'S PLEASURE BOOK.

SUNDAY PLEASURE BOOK.

LONDON: J. S. VIRTUE & CO., Limited, 26, IVY LANE.